THE ORVIS POCKET GUIDE TO
Streamer Fishing

THE ORVIS POCKET GUIDE TO
Streamer Fishing

How, Where, and When to Use this Effective Technique

PATRICK "PADDY" STRAUB

ILLUSTRATIONS BY ROD WALINCHUS

THE LYONS PRESS
Guilford, Connecticut
An imprint of The Globe Pequot Press

Although a dedication is not the norm for a how-to book, I wanted to do it anyway. This book is dedicated to my late Labrador retriever, Emma. She passed away in an unfortunate hiking accident; she was only two-and-a-half years old.

Emma, our fishing memories will be cherished, and you brought excitement and happiness into my life. Your spot in the boat will always be reserved.

To buy books in quantity for corporate use or incentives, call **(800) 962–0973, ext. 4551,** or e-mail **premiums@GlobePequot.com**.

Copyright © 2006 by Patrick Straub

ALL RIGHTS RESERVED. No part of this book may be reproduced or transmitted in any form by any means, electronic or mechanical, including photocopying and recording, or by any information storage and retrieval system, except as may be expressly permitted in writing from the publisher. Requests for permission should be addressed to The Lyons Press, Attn: Rights and Permissions Department, P.O. Box 480, Guilford, CT 06437.

The Lyons Press is an imprint of The Globe Pequot Press.

10 9 8 7 6 5 4 3 2 1

Printed in China

ISBN 1–59228–805–7

Library of Congress Cataloging-in-Publication data is available on file.

CONTENTS

Acknowledgments vii

Introduction: Why This Book Will Help You Catch More and Bigger Fish 1

1. **Predatory Trout: Their Desire to Hunt and What They Pursue** 3
2. **Reading a Stream: Where to Look and What to Look For** 26
3. **Streamer Fishing Techniques and Tactics: A New Approach to Your Fishing** 41
4. **Tools of the Trade: Equipment and Flies for Streamer Fishing** 99
5. **A Perfect Day of Streamer Fishing** 134
6. **Some Final Thoughts and the Fly Fishing Mentality** 138

Index 141

ACKNOWLEDGMENTS

For starters, I want to acknowledge everyone I've ever fished with, but I also want to single out a few fishing buddies, clients, and family friends.

Thanks to my family, especially my parents, Del and Carolyn, and my brothers, Alton and Carl, for putting up with my fishing desires and my years as a fly-fishing vagabond.

Others who deserve thanks are Brookes Morin, Jon Nehring, Garrett Munson, and Brandy Moses. I would also like the thank the following fishing clients who have allowed me to use them as "guinea pigs" for various techniques: Jeff Shrader and the whole Shrader family, Les Landau, Allen Ricardee, Tom and Becky Zavoral, and everyone else who's had the unfortunate pleasure of "riding shotgun" in my boat. Hopefully you finished the day a better angler.

A special thanks goes out to Glenn Law, who gave me my first desk job and helped me realize it was not for me. And Richard Parks will always garner thanks from me—he gave me my first guiding job. Any young guide should spend a season working for Richard.

Thanks to Tom Rosenbauer, for editing the book and giving me some great ideas. And, lastly, my gratitude to Jay Cassell and everyone at The Lyons Press for allowing me to write a much-needed book.

INTRODUCTION: WHY THIS BOOK WILL HELP YOU CATCH MORE AND BIGGER FISH

Picture this: a lazy sunrise is making its way atop the hills, and a very light breeze lifts the humidity from the river's surface. A few waxwings and finches are singing in the willows, accompanying the whir of line being pulled from your reel as you rig your fly rod. You tie on a #4 Olive Rubber-Legged Woolly Bugger and quietly wade out to the edge of your favorite riffle. With 30 feet of fly line stripped from the reel and ready, you make one false cast, shoot the line, and "plop" the Bugger down. A few strips of your fly, and *wham!* there's a heart-stopping take as a trophy trout attacks your fly. *You* are streamer fishing.

Anglers have been fishing streamers for several hundred years, ever since the Vikings tied feathers to whalebone hooks. At the turn of the twentieth century, anglers in New England fished streamers on a regular basis, but that practice still took a backseat to dry-fly fishing. Over the past sixty to seventy years, the act of fly fishing with streamer patterns has gone through many stages, having been constantly revolutionized with new patterns, tactics, equipment, and philosophies.

The Orvis Pocket Guide to Streamer Fishing defines streamer fishing as the act of using large fly patterns that imitate baitfish, crayfish, or any other trout food that is big in size, such as mice, frogs, salamanders, baby ducks, drowned birds—the possibilities are endless.

Streamer fishing, when done correctly and passionately, will result in you catching larger fish than with other methods. If I were to ask most fishing guides what method of fishing is their favorite, the responses would be almost unanimous: pounding the banks with big streamers. Nothing matches the thrill of watching a monster brown trout hunt your streamer, your breath stopping for an instant, and the toilet-bowl swirl of water from a pig brownie engulfing your fly. Streamer fishing is also, by nature, very active—you are stripping the fly more, using more specialty casts, and continually hunting for big fish. It is also very visual. Most strikes you will see or you will see a big flash in the water as a trophy slashes at your Bugger.

The Orvis Pocket Guide to Streamer Fishing is not going to make you an expert streamer angler overnight, but it will make your streamer fishing more enjoyable and successful. Most moderately experienced fly anglers have the basic skills to be successful while fishing the big bugs; they just need refinement and, perhaps, a different spin on the specialized, and very fun, techniques and tactics that make for successful streamer fishing.

Chapter One

PREDATORY TROUT: THEIR DESIRE TO HUNT AND WHAT THEY PURSUE

The typical trout stream is an environment like no other. There are fast- and slow-moving currents, deep holes, long shallow flats, undercut banks, and pocket water, not to mention ever-changing flow rates, weather conditions, and food sources. All these factors play a vital role in how a trout makes its way through the day.

On one side of the coin, trout have it made. They are able to hold in the current, expend little energy, and have their food come to them. The flip side is that larger trout—trout over 16 inches—that need substantial food to fulfill their diet, would have to eat all day long, snacking on small morsels of nymph after nymph and expending considerable amounts of energy. From years of angling experience, though, I know this is not the case.

Once trout become a certain size, they are considered predators, not foragers. A good analogy is that of a meadowlark or other songbird to that of a raptor. Songbirds excitedly fly from tree to tree, bush to bush, dashing and darting about, eating bugs and seeds. Raptors put themselves high above, either perching in a tree or flying on a thermal, as they concentrate on an area that will soon provide prey.

Fingerling trout feed strategically in lanes of current that are close to areas of cover, where, at the slightest hint of danger, they can dart for safety. As trout grow, they increase their need for a larger and more plentiful food source. During a heavy hatch, then, larger trout will naturally position themselves in a location where the most amount of food can be had, while using the least amount of energy. Ultimately, their search leads them to smaller fish. The largest trout are in a constant hunt for prey and, when not on the prowl, they are searching for a safe place to recover from their forays.

Just as a dry-fly or nymph angler targets specific water during specific times of the day or year, an angler who ventures into the exciting world of streamer fishing will ultimately target the obvious, and sometimes not so obvious, places to cast that big ugly. And the streamer angler will most likely catch the larger fish!

Location, Location, Location

I often guide successful businessmen and women. Whenever I tell them about my house, which is a modest dwelling in one of the nice neighborhoods in town, they always tell me a fact I knew long ago: With a good real estate investment, the three most important factors are location, location, location. The same three factors hold true for catching large trout on streamers.

Targeting trout on streamers requires an understanding of what trout need. Many studies have been done on where and how far a large trout may travel in a given water, and the conclusions run the gamut from a few to a few thousand yards. What are these fish looking for in their wanderings? For starters, they are searching for food, but when food is not available, then what? If not searching for food, these fish are taking advantage of cover.

"Cover" is a broad term used to describe the places where a trout may go to feel safe or to rest in between periods of feeding. It can be found in the refuge of a deep, slow pool; the shallow, cobbled bottom of a flat, where a trout can camouflage against the multicolored bottom; the out-of-sight refuge of an undercut bank; the fast current of a riffle, its broken surface making it hard for birds and other prey to see into the water; any sort of submerged or partially submerged obstruction, such as a rock or log; and anything else that creates a break from the current or limits the ability of other predators to see into the water. Understanding cover is essential because these refuges will be a primary target for the #2 Olive Woolly Bugger!

- *Deep pools and drop-offs* are the most common locations anglers look for when fishing streamers, and for good reason. These locations offer refuge to bigger trout and are common places of cover during times fish are not actively hunting for food.
- *The shallow, cobbled bottom of a flat* allows a fish to blend in with his surroundings. Often, these flats have weaker currents, where smaller fish can be more active. By camouflaging themselves in these locations, larger trout have the element of surprise and attack on smaller fish.

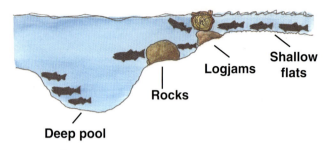

Examples of cover

- *Undercut banks* provide cover and locations from which to ambush prey. Trout will settle in under the safety of a cutbank during periods of inactivity, and undercut banks can serve up little trout to big fish holding in the same places; they draw in small fish seeking cover, and, completely oblivious to a larger predator already there, they become an easy meal.
- *Riffles* also create cover for trout. The rough surface of the water makes it very difficult for birds (and humans) to find trout. Although the current is fast, a larger rock submerged or partially submerged can create enough of a break for a good-sized fish to hold, expending very little energy. The ambush factor in a riffle is also very high: Because of a riffle's fast and noisy nature, the ability of a large trout to ambush a smaller fish is maximized. During hatches, fishing streamers through riffles can produce some *very* big fish.

Riffles

- *Physical structures* that have fallen or been placed in the water also create cover and refuge for trout. Similar to an undercut bank, a submerged or partially submerged log creates safety from above, a break from the current, and allows for the ambush factor. On western rivers, we often have a lot of deadfall or trees that have drifted down during high-water periods. These provide great habitat for large fish. On eastern rivers, exposed root systems create cover structure. Trees, deadfall, and other physical structures are most often the obvious targets for streamer anglers.

BEHAVIOR AND FEEDING RHYTHMS

Of all the species I've pursued with a fly rod, trout and tarpon share similarities in their extreme sensitivity to environmental changes. Just as a tarpon may cease rolling when a light breeze ripples the surface, trout may move from a deep hole to a shallow flat. Obvious changes, such as weather and sunlight, are easy for most anglers to notice and adapt their fishing to. However, more subtle changes, like those of water flow or river level, water temperature, light penetration, rising or falling pressure, and current hatches, all play a vital role in the feeding patterns of trout, especially large trout.

The biggest factor, and one that affects all others, is the weather. When I say "weather," I mean air temperature, wind, barometric pressure, rain or snow, and changing light conditions due to changing cloud cover. We've all heard other anglers talk about "good streamer weather"—cool, overcast, perhaps even a light drizzle. Those are good conditions, but the purpose of this book is to unlock the *myths* about streamer fishing. So, it may come as a surprise to you that some of my best streamer days occurred during bright sunlight in the middle of the summer.

Garrett Munson, a well-known guide on Montana's Missouri River, once told me why he fishes streamers almost exclusively on his days off. He said it's because, in part, that fishing the big uglies is not dependent on the weather, unlike most dry-fly situations. Prime, dry-fly fishing conditions can be ruined if an afternoon thunderstorm blows in or a hard rain takes over. However, streamer fishing is not affected by the weather nearly as much as dry-fly fishing. Even in periods of high winds, anglers can have success casting and fishing heavy, weighted flies. I'll discuss those tactics later.

We already know that big trout are predators and prefer to eat smaller fish (or fewer but larger meals). However, how does that relate to the weather? All trout are very sensitive to weather changes, but large and small fish react differently to them. For example, small fish might be more than willing to feed on a shallow flat on a bright sunny day, but a large fish may feel more comfortable resting in the shadows of a shady bank. At some point, though, that big fish is going to get hungry and seek the smaller prey. The bigger lesson here: never overlook groups of active small fish. Big trout certainly don't.

A rise or fall in water temperature would cause a big fish to give up his hiding place and pursue small fish. The normal *comfort* range for trout is anything between 40 and 68 degrees Fahrenheit, while the prime *feeding* temperatures are between 50 and 65 degrees. If the water temps are in this prime feeding range, chances are good you will be able to target actively feeding big trout. These fish must pursue food in order to maintain their metabolism.

The amount of light penetrating the water or available sunlight are other factors not to be overlooked. Oftentimes, the early morning angler gets the big trout, but that's not always the case. I have seen many waste away the morning hours, chucking big streamers with no luck, then proceed to complain of a sore arm by lunchtime. Don't get me wrong, during the heat of summer, and especially on many eastern and Midwestern streams, many big fish feed during the first-light hours of the morning. These fish may not be actively hunting and feeding as much as they will be during the low-light evening hours, but they are more likely to be in the typical big-fish haunts.

In the Rockies, with our higher elevations and cooler nights, the mornings tend to be the slowest time of the day, except, of course, during Trico mayfly emergences. You might find a few big fish foraging in the morning hours, and it is worth pursuing; however, keep in mind, big fish will hunt throughout the day and *especially* during periods of prolific hatches and on overcast days.

The wind is a variable more common on western rivers, but it is worth considering, even on the more sheltered eastern waters. Wind typically does not affect the desire of larger fish to hunt and feed. It will, however, create a few unique situations. If the breeze is enough to blow adult insects off the water's surface, smaller fish are less likely to feed during a hatch. An upside to a stiff wind is that big fish will move closer to shore in the hopes of feeding on any terrestrials blown *into* the river. Wind does make it harder to get your fly where it needs to be, but, with practice and the casting tips in this book, you will be better armed to take advantage of the distinctive circumstances created during windy conditions.

STREAMER-SIZE ME

Now that you've gained a little understanding of cover and what trout need to feel safe, you need to understand their primary food source. I often hear guides say, "Big fly, big fish." In most fishing situations, this is certainly the case. But, there are instances when smaller flies generate more success, even smaller or more sparsely-dressed streamers, and I will cover those in a later chapter. For now, though, let's follow that time-tested rule of "big fly, big fish."

First, you need to understand what large fish eat. As stated earlier, when trout grow to more than 14 inches, the bulk of their diet consists of prey large in size. But, be careful not to limit your understanding of a large trout's diet to only smaller fish. Crayfish, leeches, and hellgrammites can be food, as well as mice, small frogs, salamanders, and even birds. Remember, the trout we seek are predators and usually the largest trout in the system, so nothing is off limits.

We've all heard the river myth of a mother duck quietly swimming along, her ducklings neatly in a row behind her. But, one by one, each unsuspecting duckling disappears into the toilet-bowl flush of a big brown gulping it in. Although I've never seen this happen, small birds have been found in the stomach contents of large trout—and just *hoping* to see a sight like that is the necessary level of optimism needed to be a successful streamer angler.

BAIT FISH AND SMALLER FISH

An old wives' tale exists among the old-timers in Montana, that if you want to know what the big fish are eating, you talk to a taxidermist. However, anyone who has ever cleaned a large fish and taken the time to examine its stomach contents knows exactly what these hogs eat: other fish. Even a large rainbow trout will eat a smaller rainbow trout—the appetite of a large trout does not discriminate when hungry! They do this because smaller fish are the most available, immediate, and filling food source at that moment.

Like the tidal environment, rivers have flows that rise and fall. Baitfish move with those patterns, as well. During periods of normal flow, small baitfish live in shallow water to avoid becoming lunch for something higher on the food chain. However, when flows fluctuate due to rain or runoff, these baitfish are typically found in deeper water: In high-water periods, the increase in water pushes small fish into deeper holes; and in low-water periods, their shallow-water safe havens disappear. Large trout make use of these times to feast on plentiful prey. (Big fish will also stalk the shallows for prey during low-light conditions, when they feel more comfortable.)

Little rainbows, big browns

There is nothing in my twenty-plus years of fishing and more than ten years of guiding that proves trout are *selective* to a particular baitfish. The closest they come to being so picky is on certain tailwaters, both eastern and western, where certain days a Black Woolly Bugger out-fishes any other. Then there are days when an unweighted White Woolly Bugger catches them all and any other pattern is just trial and error. But, those examples are better explained by fish behavior and feeding patterns—regardless of the water depth big trout or their prey might be found in—in combination with a few other external factors, such as weather and stream flow or clarity.

Trout feed on streamers because our offerings look filling, because we get the fly close enough to elicit an aggressive strike (or because they are actively on the feed), and because the pattern resembles any of the many food sources that inhabit their surroundings. That's not to mock the boys in the fly shop selling you on "This is *the* Bugger to fish." They indeed know what works on their local rivers. But, in order for *you* to better understand which baitfish imitation to use, it is essential to understand the basic types of baitfish in a given river or stream.

Sculpins

Just as a hardcore dry-fly angler could draw a caddisfly by memory, any dedicated streamer angler could do the same with a sculpin. Sculpins are part of the family Cottidae and inhabit both fresh and salt water. More

Sculpin top view. Note the distinctly flattened profile and prominent pectoral fins.

than eighty species exist, but trout anglers are only concerned about the few species that are considered "mottled and slimy." Sculpins rarely grow more than 4 inches, but they are packed with protein and are poor swimmers. They are bottom-dwellers, easily identifiable by their large, flattened head, elongated dorsal fin, and oversized pectoral fins.

Sculpins are arguably the most important baitfish for trout anglers because they live among trout. They are readily available and live near the bottom, where, being the weak swimmers that they are, the slow currents make for an easy existence; this environment also lets them rely primarily on their cloaking ability to evade predators. When they do swim, it is very im-

Range of size of sculpin flies. In high water, the larger one might draw the most attention, but in low, clear water it might frighten the fish, thus the need for a smaller, more subtle imitation.

portant to understand how they do it—in short, erratic sprints of 6–10 inches, immediately followed by a quick stop—and, more importantly, how to imitate it.

Darters

Like sculpins, darters live along the bottom among the rocks and cobble. A relative of the perch family, Percidae, darters inhabit eastern rivers and a very few western rivers. They are stronger and faster swimmers than sculpins, have a more pronounced and elongated head, and are typically smaller. Darters very rarely reach 4 inches in length and are more difficult for trout

A collection of fish electroshocked from the same pool shows some large brown trout (spotted backs), large white suckers (mottled backs), and an assortment of dace, young white suckers, and bluntnose minnows. The brown trout in the photo can and will eat all but the largest suckers.

to catch; darters, hence their namesake, move in short bursts without the obvious pause of a sculpin's movement. Small streams and large rivers have considerable populations of these baitfish, but they do not compare to sculpins with regards to their percentage of a trout's diet.

Other Trout

On many southeastern streams, planted fingerlings exist with a few larger resident or wild trout, and un-

While not exactly a fry, this 7-inch yearling trout can very easily become a meal for its parents.

derstanding the importance of these smaller trout in the food chain is crucial. It can be the difference between catching trout 5–10 inches long and catching a trophy fish in the double-digit pound range. Because of the big fish's aggression and hunger, they will look to smaller trout as a food source.

Chris Dombrowski, a well-known guide, grew up fishing in Michigan where stocked trout provided ample food for large fish. Dombrowski tells stories of fishing 5- to 6-inch streamer patterns just after a stocking by the DNR—and each tale ends with a trophy trout being netted. But, even in waters where stocked trout do not make up a portion of the food supply, it is still important to understand that smaller trout are part of larger trout's diet.

On the Missouri, I've seen big browns cruising shallow water, stalking 12-inch rainbows as the 'bows sip spent Tricos. In this instance, or anytime a small fish feeding on the surface is threatened, they will, almost 100 percent of the time, head for deeper water. A tactic that many guides use to solve this angling dilemma is to fish with unweighted flies on intermediate or full-sinking lines. I will cover this more in a later chapter, but understand this: With a floating line, the more you strip in—speeding up the retrieve to simulate a fleeing fish—the higher the fly gets in the water column. In other words, it is rising, not sinking. With a sinking line, at least your fly stays down longer and appears to be going down rather than up. Why does this matter? Ask yourself this: How often have you seen an 8-inch fish jump out of the water to avoid a bigger fish? Never. They always dive down. That is why you never see a 5-pound fish eating 10-inch fish—it happens too deep down for us to witness.

Dace

Dace range throughout Canada and the U.S. Many anglers have heard of the blacknose and longnose dace, and these creatures are a favorite food of large trout. Seldom larger than 4 inches, dace are more abundant in Midwestern and eastern streams, but their imitations work well in any stream. Being weak swimmers, dace are easy prey.

The blacknose dace is one of the most common trout stream baitfish and is imitated by streamers with a dominant horizontal stripe.

Shiners

Shiners inhabit warmer waters than dace or darters. In faster waters, they will inhabit the slower, deeper pools. A little larger than dace, shiners can be up to 5 inches and have a more torpedo-shaped body in comparison to sculpins. More common in warmer waters, especially Midwestern rivers and creeks, shiners and big browns are synonymous.

Crayfish

As a kid growing up outside of Bozeman, Montana, I would spend considerable time on local rivers. The lower Madison (or the water below Beartrap Canyon

A crayfish fleeing from a predator is best imitated with a streamer.

directly west of Bozeman) was a popular spot to play hooky during the spring months. Some friends and I would load into a pickup and be on the water in less than a half hour. The focus truly was more on playing hooky than catching fish—at least until I fished the river with a well-known local guide, Duke Brown.

Duke worked for my dad at the ski hill outside of town, but his true love was fly fishing. One day, he met me and a friend at the Warm Springs access. He rigged us up with the following: For me, there was a #4 unweighted Brown Woolly Bugger and, below that, on about 18 inches of 5X, a #16 Olive Hare's Ear with no flash in the dubbing; my friend had the same rig except using an Olive Woolly Bugger and a Tan Hare's

Ear. Both Woolly Buggers had nothing flashy in them at all—just chenille, hackle, and marabou. Same for the Hare's Ear.

We pushed off with Duke on the oars, and, within five minutes, my friend was hooked into a very nice brown. We landed and released it. Within another five minutes, he was hooked up again. Both fish ate the Bugger. After releasing his second fish, Duke immediately told me to switch to an Olive Bugger and a Tan Hare's Ear. Within ten minutes, I hooked a nice brown trout. We were almost, but not completely, dead-drifting the Buggers, a deadly technique I will discuss in a later chapter.

We could not explain why one color worked and the other didn't—that's just part of fishing. But Duke certainly knew what the big fish were pursuing: the river's molting crayfish. The reason a Bugger of one color worked and the other did not might be a mystery, but we had a theory. The water was clearing from a recent mud slug. When crayfish molt, their shells are almost a bluish-purple color. Perhaps the light-brown tinge to the water made the olive look more real, whereas brown amongst brown water looks almost black.

Crayfish make up a huge percentage of a large trout's diet. Also called mudpuppies, crawdads, poor man's lobster, crawfish, or mudbugs, crayfish inhabit lakes and streams throughout the U.S. Their colors range from creamy tan to dark olive. Crayfish in most trout rivers are more available to trout when they molt, losing their shell and growing a new one. They do this many times during the course of their two- to three-year lifespan.

Crayfish are most active during low-light conditions and at night. During the day, as we did on the Madison, they can be fished quite effectively during a specific stage. For us, it was while they were molting. Crayfish patterns need to be fished along the bottom, but do not need to be restricted to the deeper pools. Patterns must be weighted properly, regardless, so that they have the correct action; similar to a shrimp or lobster swimming along the surface, crayfish will scoot through the water when chased.

Leeches and Lampreys

Most common in still-water fisheries, leeches are a prime food source for trout. Leeches are active during most hours of the day, all months of the year. From my experience when fishing leech patterns, trout tend to

Leech imitation

feed on them more opportunistically than on other baitfish or crayfish. If a leech is available to a fish, he will eat it. An analogy is that of a grasshopper to a mayfly—if a hopper and a mayfly were floating side by side, conventional wisdom on most rivers argues the bigger fish would eat the hopper. The same is true for a leech versus a nymph. One could argue that is the case with all big flies—but I've seen large trout move several feet for a well-tied and well-presented leech and not even glance at a baitfish streamer.

If seen under a microscope, a lamprey would look like a predator. Designed to latch onto smaller creatures, lampreys posses a suction cup–like mouth. Two species of lampreys are important to trout anglers: sea lampreys and silver lampreys. Both have posed serious threats to populations of trout and salmon in the Great Lakes. As adults, these two species prey on young trout.

The silver lamprey is the species streamer anglers need to understand because, when abundant, young silver lampreys are a desired food source for adult trout. Found primarily in waters east of the Mississippi, the silver lamprey is smaller than a sea lamprey and rarely grows more than a foot in length. Adult silver lampreys of more than 8 inches can, and do, prey on smaller trout.

Worms

Aquatic worms present the streamer angler with a kind of dichotomy. There are more than two hundred species of worms, and all need to be understood as a food source. Yet the techniques for streamer fishing are somewhat unrefined and resemble conventional dead-drift nymphing. Most worm species do not swim, a very important trait of their behavior. Additionally, worms are very common in trout streams during periods of rising flows—releases from dams or immediately after a heavy rainstorm—and should certainly be fished during these times. A deadly rig on rivers with changing clarity, be it clearing or muddy, is an Olive or Brown Woolly Bugger with a worm dropper. I will cover a few flies in the later chapters.

Mice, Ducklings, Frogs, and Other Morsels

Trout are predators, and big brown trout are the largest predators in their home waters. Naturally, it makes sense that a fish would eat anything that looks filling and tasty. In high school, on full-moon nights, we would "mouse" the cutbanks on the East Gallatin, oftentimes catching 4-pound browns. Either the slurp of water against the bank or the silver splash in the moonlight would signal a hit. On Slough Creek, in Yellowstone National Park, large cutthroat have been seen chasing and eating frogs; Richard Parks, long-time Yellowstone guide and owner of Parks Fly Shop in Gardiner, loves to tell stories of big cutthroat puking up frogs in the net. Anglers on eastern and southern waters tell similar stories of trout and salamanders.

Craig Matthews, a well-respected guide and author, enjoys fishing mice on the Madison, even during midday conditions. He does this for a simple reason—it works!

AGGRESSION, HUNGER, AND MAXIMIZING

Trout will smack a big fly because of hunger, aggression, or curiosity. When approaching a day of fishing on a given water, it is essential to have an understanding of the food available in that water. By knowing the types of food (and, for this book, we are talking about *big* chunks of food), we have the ability to select and properly fish imitations that increase our odds of success. But, that's not the entire recipe. We must also gain an understanding of when and why fish feed, then maximize that time by fishing with proper techniques, for example, limiting false casts to keep the Bugger in the water as much as possible. I will discuss those techniques later.

At this point, you should have a good idea of where bigger fish rest and where they pursue prey. You should also have an understanding of the various food sources big fish eat. Lastly, you've gained insight into what makes a fish strike a Woolly Bugger out of hunger and out of aggression. This last element is generally out of your control. However, mastering techniques and the having the ability to understand various fishing situations greatly increases our odds of hooking up. And refining our streamer fishing greatly increases our ability to catch bigger and more fish.

Chapter Two

READING A STREAM: WHERE TO LOOK AND WHAT TO LOOK FOR

When I look back at some of my best days streamer fishing, I distinctly remember catching fish in all types of water—deep pools, cutbanks, shelves, shallow flats, and everything in between. This chapter is meant to give a basic understanding of reading water, but the focus is on breaking down water types so you fish the best places during certain conditions. (For more in-depth stream-reading and understanding of trout lies, purchase *The Orvis Pocket Guide to Approach and Presentation* or *The Orvis Guide to Reading Trout Streams*.)

Large trout can inhabit any section of a river at any time. Because of this, we need to understand all trout lies and structure and also improve our ability to read water. As we do this, keep what you learned from Chapter One in mind: We know that big fish follow or hunt a food source. If fingerling rainbows are feeding on mayfly emergers in a riffle, the 3-pound browns will respond and stalk those smaller fish. Additionally, when a big trout's prey source is not obvious to you, knowledge of its location, such as a deep pool or cutbank, will increase your odds of a hookup. We also know that during normal conditions, big trout need just a few things: cover, the ability to rest, and the abundance of nearby food.

THE STREAMER MINDSET

I will never forget the day I "converted" two anglers from Minnesota. It was mid-June on the Missouri below Holter Dam, the world-famous tailwater section. We were expecting a good PMD hatch to occur, it did, and we were able to hook a few 10- to 12-inch rainbows. But the bigger ones just eluded us.

I mentioned it was worthwhile for one angler to fish a streamer, but both declined, saying it was too enjoyable to fish dries and besides, this was the *Missouri*. For these anglers, the Missouri was strictly a tailwater, and tailwater trout, especially during a PMD hatch, were not going to eat a streamer.

It was not until I heard the distant hoot of a fellow guide, Garrett Munson, that I decided to force a change. Behind us, upstream, was Garrett in the front of his boat, obviously on a day off and fighting a big fish. As he and his group rowed past us, he hooked another big fish in the heart of the riffle; we were fishing to rising fish at its head. Garrett's whoop-whoop was muffled by the splash of the big fish as it leapt downstream of us. "What did he eat?" I yelled across the water. "Black Woolly Bugger!" Munson shouted back. That was enough to convince at least one of the anglers in my boat. For the rest of the day, we targeted riffles, shelves, and any place else big fish might be ambushing smaller fish that were eating emerging or adult PMDs.

For a long time, my fishing had pigeonholed the Missouri: I was convinced its tailwater trout would not whack a streamer during a hatch. My clients that day were subject to the same narrow thinking until they learned otherwise: Trout are trout no matter where you are fishing and have the same feeding and holding habits regardless of the river. In this case, small fish feeding on a hatch presented a prime target for big trout, and a big ugly presented to the likely holding places of these bigger fish simply provided them with just another feeding opportunity for which they didn't have to expend much energy.

STRUCTURE

Structure is a general term used to describe logs, rocks, shelves, bridge pylons, or anything that is a physical obstruction in the water. I also classify drop-offs and ledges as structure. By nature, an obstruction in the current creates a break in flow, both upstream and downstream. This break allows a fish to rest behind or in front of the obstruction. It may also create cover, as in a large log, where a fish may rest and slightly hide under it or in the shadow it casts. Structure plays a vital role in streamer fishing, and knowing how to recognize prime spots is crucial to success.

Rocks, Boulders, and Rip-Rap Banks

Rocks are the most abundant structure in trout streams. They often make up the bottom of the stream, shape its banks, and provide in-stream current breaks and holding water. When targeting rocks for streamer fishing, I focus on a few things. First is the flow of the river. During high flows or run-off periods, my focus is on the banks. On occasion, larger boulders will slow enough current to create a lie for fish, but on rocky banks, the structure creates not only a lie (or a place to rest and pick off food), but also a place for cover. More importantly, when the water is at its highest or is muddy due to rising flows, these banks offer a hint of clarity and a break in the current. Naturally, if smaller fish are among these rocks, bigger fish will follow, patiently awaiting an ambush.

In general, fish tight to the banks. As the river current rides or pushes along a bank, it creates a "V." Part of the "V" is the bank. The other half is the line or current caused by water bouncing off the bank. Fish will hold in the "softer" or slower water in the middle of the "V."

Larger boulders—and let's consider "large" to be anywhere from about the size of a pickup truck down to that of a bowling ball—either entirely underwater or partially submerged, also create currents that hold fish. During high, muddy, or rising water, target only the biggest rocks, as they will create larger "cushions of current" for big fish. To fish these cushions effectively, plan your casts relative to the cushion. Cast across it, aiming for the outside of the opposite seam. Then, depending on what sort of pattern you are fishing, strip across the cushion. Because the fish are holding in slower water surrounded by faster water, one or two strips of 1–2 feet in length should be enough to entice a strike. If not, pick up and cast again, keeping your false casts minimal.

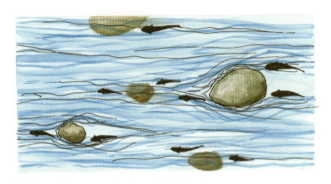

Holding patterns around rocks and boulders

Fish will also hold in front of large rocks. As the water hits the upstream side of the boulder, a small pocket is created. Fish will often hang in this break, and, more often than not, during periods of lower flows. During pre-spawn periods (fall for browns and brookies, spring for rainbows and cutthroats), I've caught many big browns in front of rocks. This is especially true in eastern streams, where the waters are generally smaller and predatory fish take up the prime feeding locations.

In low-water or normal flow periods, focus more on average-sized boulders or smaller rocks, because the clarity is better and the volume less, opening up more opportunities for more fish to see your fly. Fish can hold behind a fairly small rock; it only takes a stone larger than a fish's head to create a cushion for holding.

Holding patterns around rip-rap

Rip-rap banks are similar to regular banks, but present a unique situation for streamer anglers. "Rip-rap" is a general term used to describe any man-made or natural structure to shape or help stabilize a bank. Rip-rap can be trees cabled to a bank, large rocks bulldozed against an eroding bank, tires—even old cars, as on the Bighorn River. An on-going debate exists on the benefits of rip-rap for trout fishing success. Some anglers swear by it, others despise and ignore it. But, one thing is for sure: Spend enough time fly fishing, and you are bound to pull at least a few fish from a rip-rap bank.

Most rip-rap banks have a few common elements: current seams, back eddies, and drop-offs. Each merits differing approaches. For current seams, focus your presentations on the slower side closest to the bank.

Trout holding in a rip-rap eddy

Back eddies, or currents that boil around and actually travel upstream, are great spots to fish. Most rip-rap banks will have a large eddy at their terminus. These fish well during all flows, and especially during high-flow periods. During muddy water conditions and especially after a hard rain, look for large back eddies, whether created by rip-rap or not, to hold feeding fish. In muddy water, fish very tight to the bank, at times even stripping your Bugger off of the bank. (Remember to fish a stout leader to prevent it from becoming frayed and weak.) During lower flows and times of intense hatches, focus on the middle of the eddy, as well. Most big fish are found tight to the banks and at the head of the eddy, but I've also caught and seen the biggest fish holding just underneath smaller rising fish and at the back end, slowly working their way against the current.

Steep and fast drop-offs are also very common along rip-rap banks. Since rip-rap is usually in place to prevent a bank from washing out, faster currents hit the bank, then bounce off. This creates two things, the current seam mentioned above and a steep drop-off.

Logs and Logjams, Downed Trees, and Fences

Logs and logjams, downed trees, and fences all provide cover and a place from which large trout can ambush prey.

Similar to fishing the upstream side of a boulder, water pushing against logjams creates cushions in the current. Large trout use the element of surprise when feeding, so such structures allow these predators to hide among the branches or under the shade created by them. During periods of bright sunlight and low-flow conditions, these submerged woods will certainly hold trout. However, during high flows or when encountering

Logjams

muddy water, keep your fly away from such structure unless you can *see* the structure and strip to avoid getting snagged. If you can see the log or tree, cast to it. Don't be bashful—just be aware you may get stuck. Oftentimes it is worth the risk. In periods of rising water, such as after a hard rainstorm, I've seen many big fish pulled from underneath logs and around submerged logjams. I often say to the anglers in my boat, "High risk, high reward." Those four words of advice can work wonders while streamer fishing.

There is one instance when targeting a log is not ideal for big fish, and that's when you see a log breaking the surface, the angle pointing toward the sky. An obstruction positioned like this creates currents that cause the water behind it to rise up. Why is this a problem? It has been my experience, as well as that of fellow guide, great angler, and wonderful streamside companion, Andrew Sabota, who's fished many Midwestern streams, that bigger fish tend to like the security of deeper water. Therefore, if a current is pushing a big fish to the surface, it negates its predatory instincts, especially during high or rising flows. For months one season, Andy had been concentrating on logjams on his local Minnesota and Wisconsin rivers. After catching many large trout and smallmouth behind some logs and not behind others, he began to take notes. Soon the reason became obvious.

I've learned that big fish will hold *near* protruding logs, but typically close to the bank or a bottom obstruction that blocks the log. I also believe that in addition to feeling "pushed-up" by the rising currents behind a protruding log, they also do not like feeling so exposed in the open water column.

Larger logjams present an enigma for streamer anglers. Not very prominent on larger western waters but very numerous on eastern creeks and rivers, logjams are known for producing large fish. They provide all the elements needed for both big and small fish, but unlike a cutbank or boulder, every logjam is unique, created by numerous items mashed or jumbled together. Therein lies the mystery. But all logjams have similar characteristics.

Logjams fish well in any type of water, whether rising, muddy, clear, or low. The various structures in a logjam create a maze of cover, light and dark shadows, cushions of currents, and lots of food. On most western rivers, logjams usually occur in back eddies or on the bends. On large freestones, you may also have logjams at the head of rocky bars. After the record-high water years of 1996 and 1997 on the Yellowstone, numerous logjams delighted serious streamer anglers.

I love fishing logjams in all sorts of water, but low-water flows are the best times. During high water or runoff on western rivers, logjams, in general, have too much water flowing in and out of them for fish to hold. On slower eastern rivers, though, targeting logjams after a rain or during slightly rising water levels pays off.

Low water usually means clearer water. Therefore, a larger trout can better see to ambush your fly from farther away. But, in cloudy or muddy water, your fly must be close enough for the fish to see it, and that risks a hang-up. Again, "high risk, high reward" holds

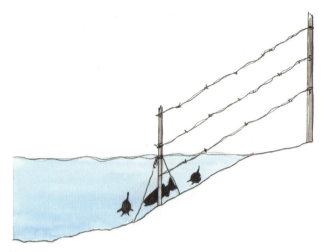

Fence lines can be productive targets.

true here, but the mixing of currents in a logjam makes it very hard to tell where or into what your fly might drift. That is why an angler must study the mess of debris before casting.

Focus on the current seams, the depth and color changes within the logjam and its contents, what structures are out of the water and which ones are not, how fast the current hits the head of the logjam—and your underlying gut instinct. There really is no right or wrong way to fish this kind of structure, but it is important to study it before you cast. It is also important to make several casts into a logjam, as it may take a few shots to entice a fish out. Grip it, rip it, and strip it.

More common on western rivers, though also a factor in other parts of the country, are fences that come up to or are even in the river, and these are worth casting to. On my home river, there are two notable "fence holes" that always hold a fish or two. I am convinced the posts create current cushions for fish to rest in. Similar to the approach for a log protruding up through the surface, fish toward the bottom of the post, as if you were trying to snag the fly where the post meets the river bottom. Big fish will almost always hang out in these places, and I've seen fish line up behind a fence post in the water column like this: biggest fish just off the bottom, medium-sized fish about 2–3 feet deep and eating emerging nymphs, and smaller fish eating dries in the surface current seam. A big fish on the bottom is in the perfect ambush situation, as it can easily come from below or behind and attack the smaller fish.

Fence lines also usually give away a gradient or depth change in the river below. We've already established that bigger fish like deeper holding water when not actively feeding. A fence line going into the water gives us an idea of where the bottom slopes down into a hole or deeper run. Fence lines also offer protection. A single strand of wire or larger posts over the water offer shelter from ospreys, eagles—and unskilled anglers.

Shelves, Flats, and Runs

Many anglers overlook the abundance of big fish that cruise shelves, runs, and flats, and for good reason, as they are usually the best water for hatches. During a

Fish holding along a shelf

non-hatch period, these areas can seem quiet, even devoid, of fish. I used to think that, until I converted my tactics to fishing streamers *first*. These places hold fish, often big fish, but they just need to be approached at the right time of day or during a hatch.

Low-light periods—dawn, dusk, and under heavy cloud cover—are prime times to strip streamers on shelves and flats. A shelf or flat in muddy water is worth fishing, but your chance for success depends on just how muddy it is. A rule that works for me and for other guides is the "18-inch rule." If you can see at least 18 inches under the surface of the water, you stand a reasonable chance of hooking up. If the water is any muddier than that, your odds greatly decrease; it is just a matter of the fish not being able to see your offering.

In normal water conditions, shelves and flats are ideal places to fish streamers. They are also the most fun; because the water tends to be shallower, you have a better chance of seeing a big fish chase your fly. If you are targeting fish preying on smaller fish, you can often see the wakes of bigger fish chasing the smaller ones. My most memorable hookups on streamers have occurred on flats and shelves and on both sunny and cloudy days. It is crucial when fishing shelves and flats that you strip your fly almost all the way back to your rod tip; fish holding in these locations will chase a fly for several yards before deciding to strike.

On sunny days, *especially* during a hatch, I spend a lot of time fishing shelves and flats. On cloudy days, I spend even more time fishing these, as bigger fish are on the prowl, actively pursuing food. This might be the time to try a mouse pattern fished close to the bank. Or the time to experiment with new retrieves—a big fish cruising a shallow flat is sure to see my #4 Woolly Bugger, but it may take the right action in the fly to illicit a strike.

Runs more than 3 feet deep can fish well in low-water periods, but require special tackle if rising fish are not seen; sinking lines and weighted flies will be necessary. Also, look for underwater structure in a run—large rocks, weed channels, or logs—as fish will rest or await an opportunity to ambush among these structures. I usually fish runs two ways, with sinking lines and heavy flies or with weighted flies and using a dead-drifting tactic.

Cutbanks, Deep Pools, Drop-offs

For reasons I hope are obvious, cutbanks, deep pools, and drop-offs are all prime locations for streamer anglers. All three offer cover and the opportunity to

Cutbank

ambush. I especially enjoy fishing cutbanks right after a rainstorm, because big fish are looking for food that has washed off the bank. Deep pools and midstream drop-offs are better fished during normal flows, but bank drop-offs, often times called "ledges" or "gradient changes," are productive during high or muddy water.

Reading water, the structure in the water, and knowing what times to fish specific water are crucial skills for successful streamer fishing. Now that you have a basic understanding of these elements, you must master the essential tactics and techniques.

Chapter Three

STREAMER FISHING TECHNIQUES AND TACTICS: A NEW APPROACH TO YOUR FISHING

I love it when I get good casters in my boat. I enjoy it even more when I get good casters who shun streamer fishing. My guiding style is not one of enforcement, none of that "You must do what I say or you will not enjoy your day" kind of attitude. It is exactly the opposite. I am all for clients setting the tone for *their* day of fishing. However, there are times when I try to sway their approach to fishing a given river or section of a river.

As is so often said after a slow day of fishing, "They wouldn't even eat a Bugger." That is because most anglers relegate their streamer fishing to the unproductive hours of the day. Most think one technique covers it all—chuck it out, strip it back, chuck it out, strip it back—and the more casts you get in the better. How untrue that is. Successful streamer fishing is a refined *task*, dare I say *art*, that requires the few essential items of solid casting ability, good dexterity, and an optimistic attitude. It may take some time and practice for the first two, but the last one is fairly easy to develop and arguably the most important. When you are fishing streamers, it is crucial to believe in each cast, that each will be the one that hooks the trophy.

This chapter will challenge your conventional fly-fishing knowledge and make you a better and, perhaps, full-time streamer angler. I am not suggesting you throw out what you've learned in the past, but I am proposing you learn a new way to skin a cat. In most of the rivers we fish, the big, old trout have seen most of our tricks. This chapter will give you new skills you can use to turn the tables on these big fish.

In the equipment chapter, I will cover the various fly lines, flies, and leaders streamer anglers will need to be familiar with. To truly target trophy trout and multiply your odds of catching fish on streamers, you will need to be comfortable fishing sinking lines. The instructions in this chapter are assuming you are moderately experienced with sinking lines, but, where necessary, I will offer pointers for their use.

GENERAL CASTING SKILLS AND PHILOSOPHY

To refine and correct your casting, read *The Orvis Fly-Casting Guide*. It will explain the basic elements of casting and define some terms. For the sake of this book, I am assuming you are a moderately skilled caster with a general understanding of the language I will be using. If you are not familiar with the terms "casting stroke," "false casting," "stripping," "roll cast," and others, touch up on your knowledge of casting skills, with some additional reading and practice, and return to this chapter.

Many anglers tire too early when fishing streamers. This is perhaps the most avoidable pitfall—even easier to solve than finding fish! Too many anglers make too many false casts. It is obvious that you cannot catch a fish with your fly in the air, but many anglers who are new to streamer fishing need to know their casts will suffer late in the day if they make too many of them early on. In short, limit your false casts and increase your odds of hooking up.

Reducing the number of false casts requires some adjustments or refinements to your basic casting skills, and that starts with the positioning of your hands. Many anglers fish with their hands too far apart. When casting, I use the two-handed axe analogy, where I imagine swinging such a long-handled tool. With the fly rod, your hands should move through the air close together—never more than 12 inches apart—because it will be

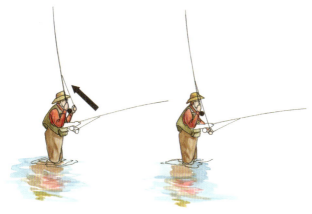

Correct hand position   Incorrect hand position

easier for you to begin stripping and mending as soon as your fly hits the water. If your line hand is at your hip when you make your presentation cast, as it most likely will be in the *wrong* position, it must travel up to your rod hand before you can start the retrieve. This dexterity is perhaps the most underrated skill of streamer fishing.

Starting a cast with the hands in the right position, it is then essential to understand hauling. A "haul" is a pull on the line by the line hand. This increases the line speed of the fly line during casts. High line speed allows you shoot your cast, drive it into the wind, or get more line out per false cast. And, in order to truly cut down the number of false casts, you must learn the water-haul pickup.

The Water Haul

The water haul begins by stripping in enough line so that you can make a backcast comfortably. With a sinking line, you need no more than 20 feet of fly line out of the rod tip and on the surface of the water. Just as you start to accelerate on your backcast, you make a small haul with your line hand; do not haul more than 4–6 inches, and, when you are done with your haul, be sure to move your line hand along with your rod through the backcast—remember the two-handed axe? You will be surprised how much line speed you can generate by simultaneously giving a short haul while you pick your line up off the water.

To continue the water haul into a triple haul, start your double haul where you normally would. After a

The water haul

quick water haul, go right into a standard double haul, and you should be able to shoot enough line so that you do not even need to false cast. In time, you will even be able to add line on your backcast, though *after* you've completed your short-but-quick water haul. This is done by unpinching the fly line in your line hand as you are bringing your rod back after the first haul in the standard double haul. It is a very quick release, but it will add 6–12 inches of line.

The water haul is a great technique that can be used with any other cast or by itself. The major drawback to the water haul is the noise that it can create. Because you are relying on the friction of the water to add tension to the line, it makes a "pop" as you pull the fly line off the water. Water hauls, therefore, are not that desirable when fishing still waters or when fishing to rising or spooky fish. During windy conditions, on the other hand, a water haul is a great technique to use because you don't need to worry about making noise—the wind is doing that for you! Water hauls are also good for fast-flowing rivers, where current muffles the noise.

The Roll-Cast Pickup and the Unsnagging Roll Cast

A roll cast is an essential cast, yet most anglers do not use it to its full potential. It has many uses: to cast line without using a backcast, to get slack out of the line before starting a cast, unsnagging a foul-hooked fly—and probably some others yet to be invented.

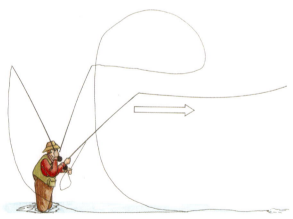

The roll cast

In simple terms, a roll cast is a forward cast without making a straight-line backcast behind you. You slowly bring the rod tip back, creating a loose arc in the fly line that extends from the rod tip down behind you, with the downhill curve of the arc touching the ground or water. The belly of the arc does not touch the ground. Once the rod tip is back and the arc created, you then accelerate and stop, like any normal forward cast.

The roll-cast pickup is essential to master when fishing full-sinking lines or sink tips, because it allows you to cast more line. If you use it, you can save yourself from having to strip most of the fly line before you can begin your backcast. With no more than 30—maximum 40—feet of fly line out of your rod tip, begin a roll cast by sliding the rod back. I've found that with sinking lines, it even helps to raise my elbow so that that the rod tip is higher in the air. You can also drift the rod tip back, giving you more room to accelerate on the forward cast. This allows for the tip to travel a greater distance on the forward stroke, but keep in mind that the movement behind is slow and gradual. You then violently accelerate the rod tip forward, forcing it into a deep bend, but stopping abruptly at the end of the forward stroke. For anglers who learned casting by the clock system, it would be approximately 10 or 11 o'clock.

A properly executed roll cast with a floating line should lay the line straight in front of you. With a full sinking line, it may take several roll casts to get the line up on the surface. Once it is, and before the line can sink, go directly into your backcast. When using the roll cast pickup with a sink tip, fewer roll casts are required, as the floating section will roll-cast easier.

The unsnagging roll cast is a must-learn for *any* fly angler, those fishing streams included. Imagine you are drifting down the Delaware River. You spot some smallish, sipping trout just off a cutbank, but your first cast is too long, landing a good foot up on the bank. As you begin to pull it off, it hooks on a log. Your guide shakes his head in disappointment, but before he can tell you what to do, throw a roll cast into the line and free the hook.

The unsnagging roll cast is simply a roll cast used when your fly is hooked on the bank and cannot be dislodged by stripping. You begin this cast like any roll cast, but I've learned that better success comes when you have less slack or "belly" in the fly line. Because you want to cast a tighter roll or loop, try to get the

The unsnagging roll cast

belly in front of rather than behind you. When you make your aggressive forward cast, it throws a tighter loop in the roll cast and is more likely to unsnag the fly. When you see the fly pop loose and free itself, make a quick backcast. In time, you will be able to perform an unsnagging roll cast, make a backcast, give a haul, and present that fly right back into the honey hole.

Depending on what you were snagged on, remember to check your leader for any nicks or cuts. When snagged on rocks, it is always a good idea to check the leader and hook point before you make your next cast. Simply run your fingers along the leader from the butt section to the fly. If you feel any abrasions, clip and re-tie the tippet and/or fly.

The Tuck or Ruckus Cast

I used to call this cast the "tuck" cast until a fishing client renamed it the "ruckus" cast. The purpose of this cast is twofold. First, it gets the fly into water at a high rate of speed, causing it to get down faster. Second, it creates a disturbance on the water, possibly attracting a trout's interest.

It begins with a regular casting rhythm. The tuck cast occurs just as the loop on your forward cast is straightening out. If your hands are in the correct position—remember the two-handed axe—it should be easy to give a slight pull or haul on the fly line. Do not make your haul any longer than 6 inches; just a quick tug will work just fine. This will slap the fly down into the water, tucking it under the leader and creating a

The "tuck" or "ruckus" cast

splash or ruckus. The tuck cast also works well with a sidearm cast, and I've seen anglers tuck the fly underneath overhanging branches and logs with this method.

The tuck cast can also be used when you've cast too *much* line and need to pull some back. For example, say you're fishing a logjam on Michigan's Ausable. You realize you've false-casted too much line, but you are on your presentation cast, the fly is coming forward, and your loop is beginning to straighten. Thankfully, you've kept your hands close enough to perform a tuck cast by pulling back on the fly line, shortening your cast just enough to drop the fly down into a little pocket of logs. A splash occurs, and, before you can get two good strips on the line, *wham!* a big brown ambushes your fly.

The Skip Cast

This cast is certainly not for purists or bashful anglers. It begins with a normal backcast, but an abrupt stop on the forward cast causes it to drive a fly underneath a cutbank or overhang. The end result should be a fly that skips as it lands on the water. The skip cast is

The skip cast

useful in getting a fly under something, because you are skipping or bouncing the fly along the surface.

To accomplish this cast, many anglers opt for a sidearm casting angle, which is just fine. However, the skip cast is not limited to this approach. To accomplish the skip cast, start with a normal backcast, but on your forward cast, overpower the acceleration just a tad. When you stop the rod on your forward cast, add a subtle flick of the wrist, something akin to flicking water off a paintbrush. This is the hardest part of the skip cast, and the timing of it should occur at the same time you stop the rod. Think about skipping a stone on a lake. When you toss a stone, your arm moves through the air, your wrists flicks, then you release the stone; there is hardly a pause between the time your arm stops and your wrists flicks. The same should be true with a skip cast. If you pause too long, the momentum of the fly through the air will die and the fly will plop on the water instead of skip. Note that cone-head, muddler, and mouse patterns work well with this cast, but patterns with rabbit fur do not skip as well.

KEEPING IT REAL: RETRIEVES AND ACTION FOR STREAMER FISHING

Now that you've gotten the fly to the water, you need to give it some action. In most situations, you should retrieve so the fly acts realistically. Hopefully, your fly pattern resembles some food source or something trout might attack. If that is the case, then the action you put into the fly becomes paramount.

Some crucial things to consider when starting your retrieves are hand position, your rod tip position, and the role of your "trigger finger." Your trigger finger is your index or middle finger, depending on where you rest the line while you strip. This is a personal preference issue, and there is no right or wrong way to rest the line. But, there *is* a wrong way to use it when stripping, and that's to not use it at all.

Your rod hand and line hand must be close enough together so that very little slack is present between them. The trigger finger can help manage this by pinching the line against the rod when needed, but I prefer to manage slack by pulling with the line hand and feeding line by twitching the rod tip. The trigger finger is sort of like the ticket taker in this whole process—it can stop the feeding or stripping at any time.

The position of your rod tip is crucial in all retrieves. It is nearly impossible to start any retrieve when the rod tip is not pointing down or at the water. If the rod tip is pointing above an imaginary horizon running parallel to the surface of the water, the rod tip becomes ineffective during the retrieve. And, if a fish were to hit while the rod tip is pointing up, your chances of getting a hook set are minimal. You are counting on the fish setting the hook himself, and, in streamer fishing, those are pretty tough odds. Most successful retrieves begin with the rod tip very close to the water. I've even seen anglers fish with the rod tip in the water, but I am opposed to this, because it limits the rod's ability to manipulate line.

When retrieving, it helps to think like the prey, as you discover which retrieve is working best on any given day. Over the years, I've never found the perfect retrieve, the method of retrieve that fish cannot resist. In my mind, retrieving is similar to casting: There are basic principles that need to be followed, but don't mess with success and personal preference. Just become comfortable with a few of the retrieves featured in this book and understand a trout's prey, and you will gain many wonderful memories while streamer fishing.

A few schools of thought exist on the speed of the retrieve, and I like to incorporate bits and pieces of each. A general rule is to have a slower retrieve in cold water temperatures (48 degrees Fahrenheit and under) and in warm water temps (66 degrees and above) and a medium to fast retrieve in ideal water temps (48 to 65 degrees). This is a very general gauge and not a hard-and-fast rule. I've had days in the middle of winter, when a super-fast retrieve caused the fish to practically jump in the boat, and similar days in high summer, when the water temps hit almost 70. Start with this general rule, but be more than willing to improvise.

The Simple Strip or Line-Only Strip Method

This is the basic stripping method used by most anglers, but it is just that—basic. It should be learned, because there are times when it is needed, but expect more action using other retrieves.

The technique is simple. Once your fly is in the water and you have proper rod and hand position—line

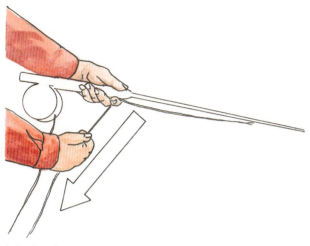

A simple strip

hand close to the rod hand and rod tip pointed toward the fly—strip in line in 4- to 10-inch strips. Longer strips can be used, especially when fishing from a boat, as you will need longer strips to move the fly if the boat is drifting toward it.

With the simple strip, you must be good at handling line with your line hand and trigger finger; if you strip longer than 10 inches, your trigger finger and line hand dexterity are critical. You must be able to quickly get your line hand back to its starting position so the fly will keep moving. Another point to note is that since there is no rod movement, it is crucial to have your trigger finger involved and sensitive to any takes.

If a fish hits during the retrieve, you must pinch the line against the rod hand with the trigger finger. If you don't, slack line will slide out of the rod as you move the rod to set the hook.

The Strip-Down Retrieve

People like the name of this retrieve because of the innuendo! But, seriously, it is a very effective retrieve. I've found it works the best when prospecting for fish or when experimenting with which retrieve will work best on a particular day. It has a nice rhythm and is somewhat meditative. It is great retrieve for fishing from a driftboat.

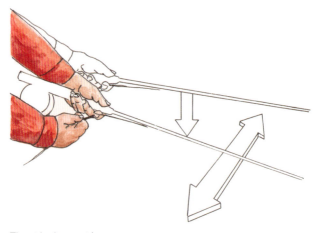

The strip-down retrieve

The basic retrieve should look like this: The fly is in the water, and you have proper hand and rod position—hands close together, trigger finger involved, and the rod pointing down to the water, toward the fly and about a foot above the surface. You give a 6-inch strip with your line hand. When the strip is complete, you lower the rod tip. While lowering, you can wiggle the rod by slowly shaking it a few times. The movement is side to side, in strokes similar to use of a pencil eraser.

The strip-down has a few minor points of refinement. The first is to strip with your line hand properly. Start your strip normally, but just at the end of the strip, put a little extra "English" on it by tilting your wrist. After this quick tilt, your thumbnail should be pointing toward the fly. Return your line hand to its position just behind the rod hand. When you wiggle the rod down, it is important that your trigger finger feels tension in the fly line. Some anglers even use their trigger finger to pinch the fly line against the rod. This is fine, but a tad risky if you get a quick strike. I prefer to have the fly line resting on my trigger finger and to control the slack with my line hand.

After you have wiggled the rod down, your rod hand and line hand should be very close together or touching. Raise them back up together about 6–10 inches and begin again. The strip-down retrieve can be fished effectively either fast or slow, but I've found anglers have better success when fishing it fast—the fly really imitates injured prey. It also works well for rivers that have large populations of darters and crayfish, because, when you squiggle the rod down, it simulates the pause in swimming so common with these baits.

The Side-Strip Retrieve

The side-strip retrieve is a variation of the strip-down, but instead of squiggling down, you "toss" the rod tip to the side. Additionally, make the strip with your line hand parallel to the surface of the water, not down, as you do with the strip-down. Similar to the strip-down, though, at the very end of your 4- to 6-inch strip, tilt your wrist a tad so that your thumbnail points toward the water. It is also OK to strip and slide the rod to the side in one motion, but I've had more success when they are two separate movements—side strip with the line hand, then side toss with the rod. Just like the strip-down, move your line hand and rod hand back to their same starting positions before beginning another retrieve.

The side-strip retrieve lends itself very well to a wide variety of fishing situations. It is a versatile retrieve that can be fished fast or slow. It is also very easy to set a hook because of your hands already being in the strip-set position. The hook-setting characteristic is a great feature when the fish are smashing your streamer. In my first years as a guide, I would watch as many anglers in my boat became frustrated with the number of false takes or charges as fish would attack their fly but not seem to eat it or set the hook themselves. This changed when I was out fishing with a friend, Brookes Morin.

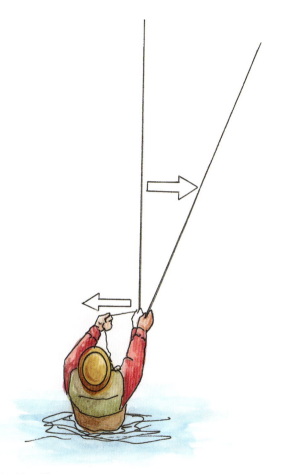

The side-strip retrieve

Brookes was trying new retrieves and attempting to master a side-strip retrieve. The fish were on that day, and Brookes continued to hook up, while my buddy in the back of the boat, Jon Nehring, struggled. It was not because Jon did not get fish to follow his fly, he was just not getting a hook in them. The reason soon became crystal clear. It was naturally easy for Brookes to set the hook, because his hands were already in the best position for the side-strip hook set. Jon, on the other hand, was stripping with a strip-down or jerk-strip retrieve and that made him raise his rod on the hook set—ineffective, and it also takes a fraction of a second longer. The difference in the time to set the hook using the side-strip method compared to another is minimal, but my experiences of fish hooked versus near misses support a side-strip retrieve when trout are aggressively attacking your fly.

The Jerk-Strip Retrieve

I know anglers who use only this method, and for good reason. Similar to the previously discussed retrieves, the jerk-strip puts great action in the fly. I am especially fond of this method when fishing rabbit fur streamers or big flies that have the ability to fluff, or "breathe," in the water after a strip. Under water, this action looks similar to a baitfish starting and stopping and will usually entice a hungry predator to bite.

Like all retrieves, the jerk-strip requires proper positioning of the rod and hands. Once the fly is in the water and your rod tip is pointing at the fly, begin the

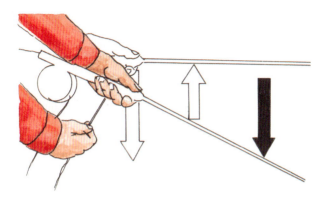

The jerk-strip retrieve

retrieve by jerking the rod downstream, or down to the water, 1–2 feet; the rod tip ends low, almost pointing in the water. By moving the rod tip a distance this great, the fly is moved in an erratic manner, thus imitating injured or frightened prey. After lowering your rod, raise it back up to your starting position, *while stripping in the slack line with your line hand.* Then, return your line hand close to your rod hand and repeat the steps. Be sure to keep your trigger finger involved when lowering your rod and while stripping in the excess.

The jerk-strip creates a very lifelike action in the fly, is easy to learn, and creates a good rhythm that makes streamer fishing quite enjoyable. And although the jerk-strip can be fished fast or slow, most success comes from fishing it aggressively. A violent jerk down combined with quick, short strips can also move the fly, making it nearly irresistible to large trout. It is also more versatile than the other retrieves discussed because it has two distinct parts: the jerk down and the strip. You can make the jerk down fast and violent, but then slow the strips. This is useful because the jerk down moves the fly enough to get a fish's attention, and being able to strip either fast or slow makes it deadly because it will work with what the fish want.

The Saltwater Jack Retrieve

This is a very specialized retrieve, one that can be quite useful at times. Its roots lie in the saltwater canals of south Florida, and it is named after the jack crevalle, a distant relative of tuna and permit. I often take my 5-weight, after pursuing permit and tarpon all day, and fish in the canals for them (or, if I'm lucky, a

The saltwater jack retrieve

snook or two). Jack are extremely fast swimmers and require a fast retrieve. Surprisingly, I've found the retrieve I use for jacks also works well in certain trout fishing situations.

The "jack" retrieve begins like the others, but once the fly is in the water, place the rod in your right armpit (or left, if you are left-handed). Strip line by alternating the hands, and do it very fast—imagine you are pulling in a rope as quickly as you can. Not only will this retrieve elicit some violent takes, it is also a hectic challenge to get the rod out from under your armpit before slack develops in the line and the fish escapes!

I've had lots of success with this retrieve when fishing shallow flats or low-water riffle corners, and it is best fished with unweighted flies on intermediate sinking lines. Also, try this on rivers where fish gather in pods and sip small dry flies. Cast beyond the pod and strip the fly through or just in front of the pod, as the largest fish often holds the first place in line.

Other Retrieving Techniques

"Jigging" is not a word usually associated with fly fishing, but I find I jig my fly fairly often. In between the various other retrieves, tossing a few jigs in the action can illicit a strike. You jig a fly by raising and lowering your rod, make a movement similar to pumping a keg of beer. When jigging, you must keep the trigger finger involved and be ready to set the hook at any moment. Heavy, weighted flies work the best for

The belly retrieve

this method, and most fish will hit when the fly is dropping, so anticipate it—the ambush happens fast. Jigging is also a deadly technique when dead-drifting streamers.

To belly or not to belly? There is an ongoing debate among many streamer anglers regarding the benefit of letting a downstream belly build in your fly line as you retrieve. My personal experience, and that of other guides, supports both sides of the fence. Anglers who let a belly develop argue it presents the fly as swimming downstream, imitating fleeing prey, and the belly creates constant tension so that the fish is more likely to hook itself. Anglers who mend and fish a straight-line retrieve argue a fish swimming downstream is a little unnatural, because most fish hold facing upstream. They also say that prey will usually swim *away* from a predator, not into its mouth. Another argument against letting a belly build is that if you are fishing a fast retrieve, the speed of your retrieve combined with the belly pulling against the current causes the fly to speed through the water almost too fast for a fish to attack.

Letting a belly build or not build will always be debated, but it is best to experiment and adjust your fishing accordingly. If you feel you are not getting strikes because the fly doesn't stay in the zone long enough, try keeping the belly out with an upstream mend to slow your retrieve. If you've had a few hits but no takes, take the belly out with an upstream mend and strip with the same pace. If you're getting looks but no strikes, let the belly develop downstream before you strip and then strip to beat the band—this will increase the fly's speed and maybe entice an indecisive trout.

The retrieve is a crucial part of streamer fishing, more important than casting. If you can get the fly to the fish but cannot make it look real, you reduce your odds of hooking up. A diverse arsenal of retrieves gives you many techniques to choose from, and that is what will really set you apart from being an angler who dabbles in streamer fishing versus an angler who can catch fish on streamers in any situation.

STREAMER FISHING TECHNIQUES

I am sure the anglers in my boat get sick of me telling them that fly fishing is a process. There are so many variables that often I am amazed we are ever able to fool trout with offerings of feathers and steel. You must cast properly, have good presentation, and offer a fly a trout wants to eat. Without even considering reading the water or having the right equipment, you must be proficient in a few basic skills to have a shot at success.

However, over the past twenty years, and especially during the past decade, we've revolutionized our sport so much in our favor that it is surprising to us when we *don't* catch fish. The advancements in gear, rods, boats, fly-tying materials, and other essential elements of fishing have made streamer fishing less work and more play. These days, streamer fishing is more than just "chucking and ducking." It is a collection of skills that will challenge your conventional fly-fishing techniques and broaden your enjoyment of our great pastime.

Effectively fishing streamers is more than just knowing a few casts and where to put the fly. Just as a dry-fly angler must focus serious attention to presenting a #18 Elkhair Caddis, a streamer angler must posses the tools to present a #2 Muddler Minnow.

THE SWING, OR ACROSS-AND-DOWNSTREAM METHOD

This is the traditional method most anglers use when they envision fishing streamers. It is fairly easy to learn, can be very effective at times, and allows for lots of improvisation with mends and retrieves. The swing or across-and-downstream method (from here on out, I will call it the swing method) is a great way to cover a lot of water in a little time. It is a favorite choice among wading anglers, but I am not a fan of the swing method for small-stream angling. For larger rivers, the swing method will produce small- to medium-sized fish or any big fish hunting for food, but it is unlikely this method will produce the largest fish in the river, as the swing method doesn't account for a trout's desire to ambush its prey.

The swing method begins with any of the casts discussed earlier, but a traditional or tuck cast is usually best. Aim your cast directly across the stream at a 90-degree angle to the current. On a small stream, aim as close to the bank as possible. If you hit the bank, slowly strip your fly off of it. Hand position is basic:

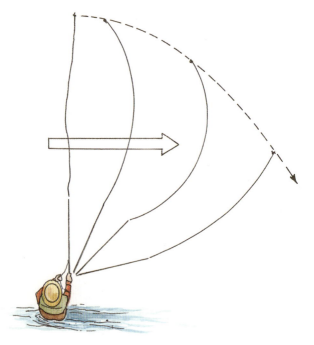

The across-and-down swing

rod hand pointing the rod to the fly, trigger finger with the line draped over it, and the line hand close to your rod hand and ready to strip.

To fish the classic swing method, let a small belly build in the middle of your fly line. Tension on the line will pull the fly downstream. Most times you'll let your fly swing across the entire line of current. If a fish hits, most likely it will set the hook itself because of the tension caused by the belly in the line. To get more out of this method, vary the speed of the swing and use any of the retrieves I've already covered. Many fish are caught using this basic method, even big fish. But I am not a real fan of the traditional swing without adding some action to it.

When wading, you can use the swing method to effectively fish pocket water, deep holes, and even logjams. This is accomplished by placing upstream mends in the fly line or by raising and lowering the rod to place the fly in the desired location. Cast close to the opposite bank. As soon as the fly lands, put a medium-sized upstream mend in the fly line and leader; it is OK if you move the fly. If there is a logjam or large boulder downstream, manipulate the drift so the fly will be stripped directly in front of the obstacle. If the fly is not on the right path, use a large upstream mend to change the drift of the fly. You can also strip the fly to get it where you want if you have cast beyond your target. Once the fly is directly in front of the structure, experiment with your retrieves. I've seen many big fish caught by anglers who simply jig or dabble the fly in front of a log or boulder.

STACK MENDING

Another technique to be used with the swing method is stack mending. Stack mending is accomplished by pumping several mends in the fly line before it gets pulled in the current and before the fly starts to move.

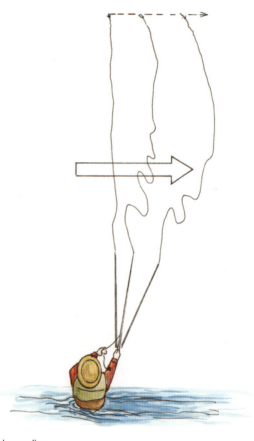

Stack mending

Begin your cast in a manner similar to the previously discussed swing drifts. Just as your fly hits, make large, sweeping, upstream mends, letting fly line slide from your fingers. Try to stack the line in large coils slightly upstream of where your fly landed.

While you are stacking the fly line, the fly is dead-drifting just off the bank. Unlike a normal swing drift, by stacking the line, your fly will hang off the bank for a few seconds more. This added time might be just enough to get a big fish to hit. Stacking line also pays off later in the drift: since the fly is not being pulled by the current, it is able to sink, getting down to bigger fish. Once you have stacked enough line, which depends on the speed of the current (but four to five big mends is plenty), follow the end of your fly line with your rod tip. Your fly is now dead-drifting along the bottom and, yes, a fish may hit it, so pay careful attention to the end of your fly line. It if stops floating, dips underwater, or does anything erratic, quickly set the hook. This hook set, one where you have lots of slack fly line on the water, is best accomplished by a side-strip hook set. If you have lots of slack, quickly side strip in all the slack until you get a tight line—it may require several strips—almost as if you were retrieving a fly.

Another deadly application of stack mending is when swinging a fly across a deep pool. Standing either at the side of the pocket or directly upstream, drop your cast well upstream of the deep pocket in the middle of the pool. Begin stacking your fly line immediately. This allows the fly to get down and drop into the deep pocket. Without stacking, the fly would drift well above the fish.

As the fly gets farther downstream from you, the mends will come out, causing the fly to rise and swing toward the tail to the pool. Most pools have a gentle upslope at their tail. This gradual gradient change is a preferred hangout for big trout. Since you stacked slack line early in the cast, the fly will swing directly in front of some of the pool's largest fish.

I've had a lot of success fishing deep holes on small creeks with this method. It is especially effective when a heavy hatch occurs and small fish are at the head of the pool eating dry flies on the surface—the big boys are submerged, like U-boats, awaiting wounded or smaller fish. There is no perfect retrieve for this technique, but I've found the jerk-strip to be the most successful.

Dead-Drifting

That day on the Madison with Duke Brown opened up a new door to me. Until then, I subscribed to the school of thought that Buggers must be stripped and streamers must have action. But by understanding a trout's food source, we see they often eat food that is not actively swimming but is rather just floating the current. This is especially true in the days before a salmon fly hatch, the several times a year crawfish molt, nights before a Hexigenia hatch, or when any other large food morsels are abundant. Whether you are in Utah, Wisconsin, or Maryland, at some point on

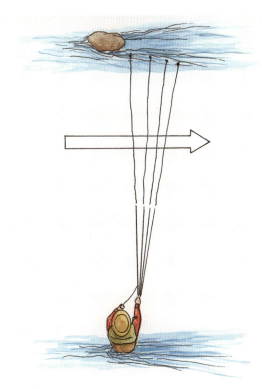

Dead-drifting

your local stream you will have a time when dead-drifting streamers is the best way to fish.

Dead-drifting big flies is nothing new, but few anglers realize the method's potential. It's just another way to describe getting a drag-free drift with the fly and fly line, while under the water, "dead" means no movement. The technique is similar to certain nymphing techniques, but varies, I believe, because streamers should not be dead-drifted with an indicator. (When streamer fishing, you need to be able to fish at different depths, and an indicator creates unnatural movement when you retrieve the fly.) Accomplishing a good dead-drifting technique with streamers also requires all the skills involved in dry-fly fishing, but requires more imagination, because you *must* read the surface of the water to decipher the structure below it. Where there is visible structure, it is easy to see where to dead-drift your fly, but when there isn't, then it requires the angler envision it.

Dead-Drifting Two-Fly Rigs

Fishing two flies at the same time is possible when dead-drifting, but is very difficult if you cast and retrieve streamers in the conventional method. Dead-drifting two-fly rigs with one big streamer and one smaller nymph works great in southern tailwater rivers and on larger western freestones at sunrise in midsummer. I am also a big advocate of two-fly dead-drifting on heavily pressured waters.

It is important to adjust your casting when fishing two-fly rigs. Cast a larger loop to keep the flies from tangling. It may take a while to get used to casting a #4 Woolly Bugger with 18 inches of dropper tippet and a #12 Bead-Head, but keep your false casts to a minimum and cast a wide loop.

When dead-drifting a two-fly rig, have your rod tip follow or track the end of the fly line and keep it parallel to the surface of the water. This will help set the hook faster, make it easier to mend, and allow for a more natural drift. If your rod tip is pointed down or angled into the surface of the water, your ability to get a natural drift is compromised. If you see the fly line stop, dive under, or do anything erratic, set the hook with a quick, side-strip hook set. If you set by *raising* your rod and it is *not* a fish, you'll pull your flies out of the water, and then you'll have to recast the cumbersome rig again. Keep those flies in the water!

Whether you are fishing a two-fly rig or just a single streamer, when you feel you've reached the end of your drift and are ready to cast again, raise your rod slowly, as if you are trying to tease a fish off the bottom; adding a jig or two might entice a strike.

Another way to increase the odds of getting a hit is to let your fly line swing to the end of the drift before you begin a new cast so that the fly rises to the surface. Play around with various retrieves—you just never know what it takes to get that 3-pound fish to eat. I've had days when my anglers tried all the retrieves in the book—dead-drifting Buggers, prospecting with dries, and nymphing with indicators—but the only fish we caught were hooked when those anglers slowly lifted their flies through the water before casting again. This technique is very similar to the Leisenring Lift used with wet flies and nymphs—however, if it works, I'll call it whatever anyone wants!

DREDGING OR DOING THE "DOWN-AND-DIRTY"

There is a slight difference between dead-drifting and what some anglers call "dredging." I prefer to call the dredging technique "down-and-dirty" streamer

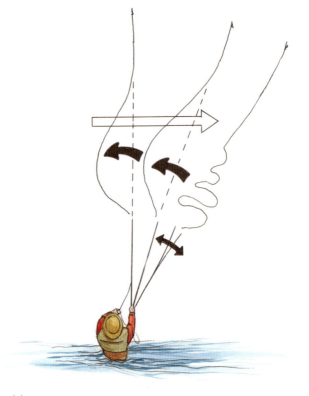

Dredging

fishing—dredging sounds too much like something done in the Mississippi Delta, not on your favorite trout stream.

This method is not for the faint of heart, as it requires patience, nontraditional fishing equipment, and lots of imagination. It is called down-and-dirty for obvious reasons: you fish down, and you are using "dirty" or ungentlemanly methods.

To dredge effectively, you need to use sink-tip line. Mending is crucial, since you are drifting the fly rather than stripping the fly. A down-and-dirty drift is similar to a dead drift, but the presentation is more focused and requires a commitment to fishing it with a specialized line and systematically covering a large, deep hole. This is the primary method to imitate dead or dying minnows.

There are a few other basic differences between dredging and dead-drifting aside from the fly line used. The main difference is in how you present the fly. After talking with many anglers and taking in my own fishing experience, I've found down-and-dirty drifts are more successful when you get the fly drifting downstream, head-first. This is best accomplished by pumping in a large upstream mend as soon as the fly lands, and it requires several more upstream mends with the floating portion of the fly line. Keep the sink-tip portion of the fly line from moving and *only* mend the floating section, because any movement in the sink-tip will pull at the fly, creating an unnatural drift; you may also have to feed slack line out of your rod tip to keep the drift going and to keep the fly from rising to the surface. As the fly approaches the end of your drift, lower your rod to give a little more slack, tracking the floating portion of the fly line. ("Tracking" is pointing your rod tip at the end of the fly line and following its drifting with your rod tip.)

When finished with the first drift through a deep hole or run, make several more, systematically covering the entire pocket. Down-and-dirty fishing is not about relying on predatory fish to actively pursue and ambush your fly, rather it is a searching method designed to find resting or holding trout. Reading the water is very important and so is strong concentration, as you must imagine what your fly is doing 4–10 feet under the surface—all while fishing with unbounded optimism that a big fish will strike.

When a strike occurs, I prefer the side-strip strike method for the same reasons I like this hook set when dead-drifting. It does not pull the fly up, and you can quickly get slack out of the line.

Two-Fly or Tandem Rigs

As I discussed earlier, dead-drifting two flies is a great way to catch trout. However, I did not talk about fishing two *large* flies at the same time. I use this tactic quite regularly on our larger western rivers. I am sure that it would work on other waters in the U.S., so give it a try on your local water.

Effective two-fly streamer rigs

STREAMER FISHING TECHNIQUES AND TACTICS

I like to fish at least 10 inches of tippet for the dropper fly, and I usually fish a brighter, more visual fly topside, with a darker fly as the dropper. This solves two problems: First, you can see the lighter fly, so you get the thrill of seeing a fish follow and take. Second, you are able to cover two schools of thought on the same cast—you get to fish a light fly and a dark fly, so you have both color spectrums represented.

Various knot leader systems can be used for this method. The most common is to tie the first fly on with a clinch knot, then the dropper tippet onto the bend of the hook of the first fly with a second clinch knot. Tie the second fly onto this dropper tippet with a third clinch knot. Another rig I use quite often is a dropper loop in the leader above the first fly. The second fly gets tied onto the dropper loop with a piece of tippet that is looped on one end—the fly is on the other. The dropper loop makes it easy to change flies without have to retie the whole rig. The third rig I use when fishing split shot or sink putty. I add two 10-inch sections of tippet material, leaving about 12 inches of one tag end in each of the blood knots. On those tag ends, I tie my flies. At the end of the last tippet section, or end of my line, I add the weight.

Obviously, casting is tougher with two big flies, but with practice, it will feel the same as fishing a big Bushy dry and a Bead-Head dropper. At first, try throwing a wider-than-normal loop. If it is still difficult, try fishing a weighted fly for the first fly and an unweighted Woolly Bugger for the second.

HOOKING AND FIGHTING BIG FISH

I've already covered the various ways to set a hook when you see or feel a fish strike. My favorite method, time and again, is to set a streamer hook with a side strip—very similar to setting the hook on tarpon. When you see or feel the fish, strip-strike by making a hard, 8- to 12-inch strip with your line hand and driving the rod to the side and slightly down, spreading apart your line and rod hands. It may take two or three strip-strikes to really drive the hook home.

Once hooked, big fish typically have two reactions: either entire pandemonium breaks loose, like kids at a circus cash-drop, or you feel a very strong, deliberate pull, not unlike hooking a large log. The latter probably means the fish is not really sure what is happening—at least not yet. When it *does* figure it out, you will be glad you learned some basic principles of fighting big fish.

The first of these principles is to understand why a fish does what it does when hooked, and despite our efforts to humanize big fish and their reactions to being hooked, it's all about survival instincts. A big brown trout does not *consciously* dart under a log when hooked, causing a breakoff. Nor does it "think" to burst out into the middle of the river to jump and toss the fly. It is merely following its natural instinct created by the fear of not knowing what is going on.

We can combat this if we understand one key element: a fish *must* go where its head goes. This is not a groundbreaking idea. Anglers have known this for

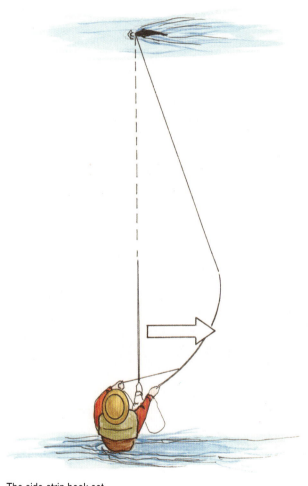

The side-strip hook set

years. However, many have failed to properly take advantage of this principle. Two things are key to getting the upper hand when control of a fish's head is at stake: knowing and using your equipment effectively and understanding the role river currents play in the battle.

Equipment

First, the role of your equipment. Modern fly rods are quite marvelous tools for casting to and fighting big fish. Manufacturers tout rods with different actions, flexes, and tapers. I've found that any rod will work to apply the pressure necessary to tire a big fish. But there's more to your rod when it comes to using it most effectively.

If you want to control the head of a fish, pull it in the direction you want the fish to go. The best way is to use the butt section of the rod. Lower the angle of

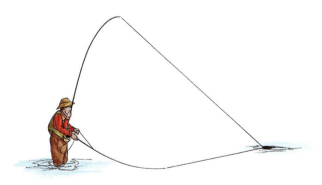

Rod angle

your rod so it is more parallel to the surface of the water or to your side and down, similar to the position your rod should be when you strip-strike the fish. This allows the strongest part of the rod, the butt section, to apply pressure on the fish.

When fishing streamers, we usually fish thicker or stronger tippets than in other fishing situations. In most instances, we risk pulling the fly out of the fish rather than breaking the fish off—hence the reason we are able to use the butt section of the rod instead of the tip. This is accomplished by finding the rod angle that gives us the best leverage with which to apply steady, even pressure, but one that still allows us to feel movement of the fish's head. That rod angle is almost always to the side and nearly parallel to the water. Occasionally it is

Rod tip action

higher, but only in situations when the fish has control of its head and we are unable to change it because we risk losing it (as is the case when a fish changes direction quickly and makes a hard run downstream).

If the rod is perpendicular to the surface of the water or above us, we are only controlling the fish with the last few feet of the rod tip—the weakest section of the rod and the section with the most amount of play. As soon as you change the angle of the rod, lowering it to the side, you will notice less bend in the tip and will feel you've gained more control of the fish's head. Be very careful in this instance, however, never to have the rod pointing directly toward the fish. This is a hard adjustment to master because a big fish can change direction fast. If you point the rod straight at the fish and let the rod get low or close to the surface of the water without a sideways angle, the chance of popping the fly out or breaking the tippet increases.

If a fish *does* get control of its head and runs downstream, let it go by raising the rod so it is perpendicular to the water and apply slight but steady pressure on the reel. Hopefully, you set the hook well enough on the strike so that the pressure of the reel is enough to keep the hook in—it should be, as the reel drag and the pressure of the fly line in the water is fairly strong. However, as in most sports, defense is not the time to rest, so be ready at any moment to win back control of the fish's head during its run. When you feel it slow down, stop, or raise up in the current, you can then lower your rod back to the sideways angle and apply side pressure again.

Using River Currents

Most anglers first learn how—and how not—to use their rod to aid in their fight with a big fish. After you've mastered the feel of fighting fish with the rod, you then need to understand how to better use the river currents to your advantage for tiring a fish. You also sometimes need to know the currents to determine when to let up during the fight. As in any battle, knowing your opponent's weaknesses and exploiting them when you can is crucial to victory.

A trout's movement in a river is primarily dictated by current. They cannot stop suddenly, they do not have a reverse gear, and their head controls their path. Understanding these three facts stacks the deck in your favor if you stay focused on the fish and what it is doing. Yes, there are variables in the equation, such as your tippet strength, structure in the water, your ability to tie good knots, the position of the boat, the boat's oars, how many beers you've had, and so on. But, knowing the basic positions a trout takes when hooked can put you back in the game with the momentum in your favor.

- *A fish running at the angler* presents a precarious situation, and few things in fly-fishing are as thrilling. This circumstance requires quick thinking and fast hands. First, you must get any slack out of the line by stripping with your line hand. Then you must make a quick decision on which way to add side pressure when you detect a slight slowdown in the fish's run. In most cases, you

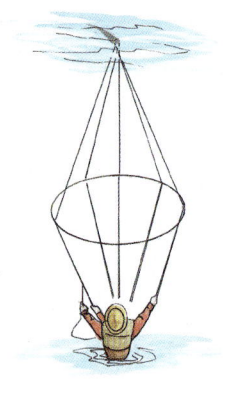 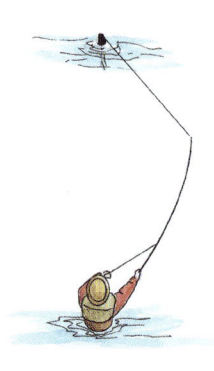

Fish-fighting tactics

will want to pull its head sideways, down, and toward the river's slowest current, usually back toward the bank. If the fish will go, great, but it will probably feel safer in the deeper water of the middle and will fight your pull. Early in the fight, the fish will probably not raise its head but will instead keep it down, trying to get deep. *Don't* let the fish turn a 180 and head downstream.

- *If a fish is running away from you*, whether directly downstream or across the currents, you are at its mercy. Raise your rod so it is perpendicular, but not too high above your head. Keep the rod butt lower than your chin and you will have better control, plus it is easier to put side pressure on the fish if it stops running. You can add to your defense by moving with the fish, either downstream or

STREAMER FISHING TECHNIQUES AND TACTICS **87**

stepping out in the current (but be very wary of wading out too deep, as the deeper you get, the stronger the force of the water is against your body), because doing so helps you gain ground when you regain control of its head. If you are in a boat, get your buddy on the oars and chase the fish. You can also increase the drag of your reel, but this is a nitpicky point with some anglers. Many anglers feel you should never adjust your drag with a fish on, but I feel differently. If you are able to watch the fish, feeling the fish with your rod hand, and can tighten or loosen your drag, then do it. Loosening your drag is certainly worth considering the farther away a fish gets, because the more water pulling on your fly line, the greater the tension.

After a fish makes a long run, whether straight downstream or across, it will most likely take a second to gain its bearings and hold or rest in the current. At this moment, go on the offensive and attempt to take control of its head. The battle is now neutral, and it is up to you to make a move or risk having to react to the fish. Similar to a fish running at you, you need to choose a direction to apply side pressure. Try for one where the current is less, and don't be afraid to pull the fish first one way and then quickly the other, being aggressive when you change directions so the fish never has a chance to regain its vital head control. If the current is strong, only steady side pressure is needed, and you may not need to change the direction that often. If the current is slow, pull the fish to the right for a few yards; then, if and only if you can turn it, pull it to the left for a few yards. If at any time during this part of the fight the fish turns aggressively toward the bottom and tries to burrow in the deeper water, ease up on the pressure.

- *A fish diving toward the bottom or burrowing* presents a unique situation. In this instance, the fish has control of its head and is turning away from you. Treat it similarly to when a fish is running directly away from you, being ready for the moment the fish stops and you can regain head control. However, this burrowing behavior usually

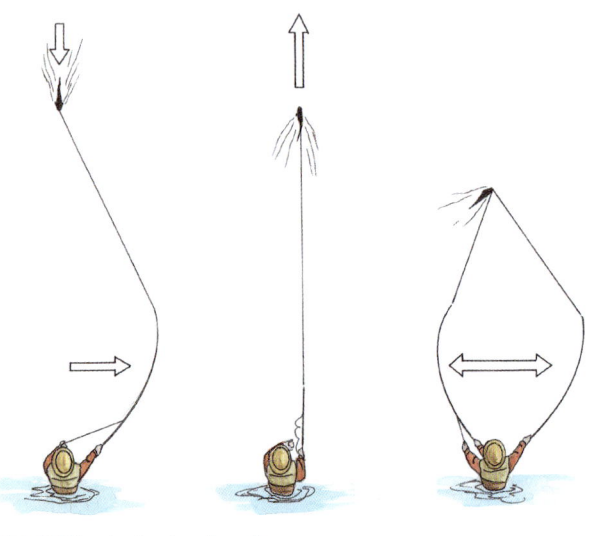

Fish-fighting tactics (continued)

STREAMER FISHING TECHNIQUES AND TACTICS   **89**

happens when a fish is very close to you or even heading upstream of you. Do not try to force its head up, as this will certainly pop the fly or break the tippet. You can, however, lean out with the rod toward the fish by extending your arm. Once your arm is extended, try making a very large circle with the fly line to slowly turn the fish in a circle—you just might be able to get it pulling against the current, tiring itself in the process. Or, better yet, it might rise up, its head moving toward the surface and turning the fight back in your favor.

- *A fish with its head rising up or facing up* to the angler is the best scenario when a big fish is on the line. Current pushing against the fish causes its head to rise and makes it more difficult for the trout to turn down or in another direction. You can also add side pressure in this situation to tire the fish, but be sure to not add too much of it down or the fish will get its head turned down. In this instance, you are in the driver's seat. Most likely the fish is tired and ready to be landed, so keep steady pressure, using as much of the rod as you can. If you feel the fish pause or give, keep pressure on its head where you can control it—even if that means turning the fish—but be sure to not pause as you change angles. If you are alone, try to gain line and get closer to the fish, as once you are able to truly get control of a trout's head, you can get a net under it easily. (I instruct anglers that once they see a trout's nose break the surface, they should net it. If you are in a boat with a fishing partner, this job is much easier.)

LANDING YOUR TROPHY

You've spent all this effort to cast, present the fly, hook, and fight a monster trout. Now it comes time to land it. Landing fish is often the most overlooked aspect of fly angling, but that's because there are so many theories on how to do it. (I hope you practice catch-and-release fishing, but if even if you don't, you still have to land the fish before you get it in the pan.) Some anglers swear by nets, others do not. I've seen many anglers lose fish while fumbling around without a net, but also I've seen far too many fish suffer because anglers did not use one, so I believe in using nets to land fish. That being said, for fish that are going to be released, it is crucial anglers use one of the nonabrasive net bag materials that are on the market. Rubber net bags are the best.

Always try to net a big fish when you are sideways to it. You can do this easily by keeping control of its head and steadily pulling the fish about 1–3 feet under the surface of the water. Pull to the side and slightly upstream. Once the fish is a tad bit upstream of you or the side of the boat, get your net ready. Have it positioned behind or to the side of the fish, with the outside edge partially submerged. Try to scoop the fish up, as if taking a shovel of gravel without spilling it. Avoid stabbing the water while netting—this will only spook the fish and make you look silly.

STREAMER FISHING TECHNIQUES AND TACTICS

Do *not* net a fish by holding the net directly upstream of it while trying to pull the fish perpendicular to the line of current. Netting a fish this way increases your odds of breaking off the fish, and it is also very hard on a big fish because it forces water violently and unnaturally through its gills. Many anglers also like to try to net the head of the fish, and this is a good approach. But if you do not follow the steps above and approach the net job from the right angle, it will be hard to get the fish in the net. Whether you aim for the head or the midsection, it is important to have control of the fish's head first, and then come at the fish from the side or underneath.

If you are not using a net, it is very important to control the fish's head before you reach down for the tail or to cradle the belly. If you choose to beach a fish that you plan to release, do it gently and in an area that is not muddy. Stirring up mud or sand gets it in the gills and can suffocate a fish. Think gentle thoughts if you are not using a net. I am against tailing, because that requires a fish to be very tired before you can get close enough to grab it without spooking it, and it is just plain difficult to grab a large fish's tail—they generate all their power with it, and it's strong. I think the best way to land a fish by hand if you're going to is to place your rod in your armpit, making sure to leave slack in the line to avoid breaking the rod tip, and use two hands, one to gently cradle the fish's belly and the other to grab its back just before the tail. Try to gently roll the fish to its side, as this may help disorientate it, and perform the entire operation while keeping the fish in the water. You will also find it much easier to land a fish by hand if the fish is upstream of your position.

PHOTOGRAPHING FISH

I was in the Bahamas one winter, and I was having a cold Kalik after a day of bone fishing, my mind at ease, my nose a little sunburned, but enjoying a simple fact of the angling life: fly fishers pursue fish in some of the most beautiful places on earth. For this reason, I think it is important to have a small section on photographing your fish.

A few general principles should be followed: First, keep the fish in the water as much as possible. Second, fish pictures are always better the closer the fish is to the water. Third, make sure the angler *and* camera operator are ready. Fourth, take your sunglasses off for a picture—let your friends see the great expression on your face! Fifth, raise, click, and lower—quickly raise the fish for the picture, shoot the photo, and immediately let the fish breathe in the water. And last, smile and enjoy your picture.

RELEASING BIG FISH

Properly releasing fish is another overlooked aspect of our sport. The key to a fish's survival exists the moment you hook it. By using the principles above, you are now able to quickly land trophy trout, but don't let all the skills go to waste by not releasing one properly.

Release a fish in water where it can rest behind structure, either a submerged rock or log. Be sure to release it upright, with its head facing upstream, as this allows water to gently pass through its gills. Do not release fish in water that is very fast or too slow, as they need to be able to rest but with enough water flowing to replenish their depleted oxygen supply. If needed, revive a fish by facing it upstream in gentle current and moving it back and forth; when you feel the fish ready to go on its own, release your grip. If you release a fish and it stays under the boat or behind structure and does not move after 5 minutes or so, flush it out by walking toward it or poking your net handle near it. As the fish swims away, be sure to savor the moment and look around you—you were paying so much attention to the big fish on your line you might have missed the osprey in the tree, the moose gnawing willows, or the bear scrambling down the bank.

UNHOOKING YOURSELF

If you have not figured it out already, streamer fishing requires a different mindset than other means of fly fishing. It also requires bigger, heavier flies. Hopefully, you are able to limit your false casts, but sometimes your perfect false cast might perfectly hook your ear or your fishing partner. When this happens, there's no need to panic, just learn this time-tested method for removing embedded fish hooks.

The first way to make an unhooking job easier is to fish barbless hooks or at least pinch the barb before you begin fish. (I even believe a barbless hook sets better in a fish.) To release a hook from yourself or a partner, push down on the shank of the hook to disengage the barb or slightly offset the angle of the bend. While pushing down, pull straight from the bend of the hook. For hooks that are in deep, get a piece of strong monofilament. Loop the mono around the bend of the embedded hook. With one hand, push down on the middle of the hook shank to disengage the barb and, *at the same time,* pop the hook out by pulling on the monofilament in a line exactly parallel to the path of entry.

SPECIAL TACTICS FOR FLOAT-FISHING AND WADING SITUATIONS

I won't say that a true streamer angler must float-fish a river, but it does help on certain waters and during certain times of the year. Floating a river allows you to cover more water, fish both banks, and can make casting easier. The drawbacks are you have to be better at line handling—your line and rod hands must work together more efficiently—because you have less time to fish a given spot.

But, perhaps the biggest difference between wading and boat fishing is that when wading, you are limited in your ability to fish banks properly. You can successfully fish both banks on smaller rivers or creeks, and, for many eastern and southern anglers, this is the case. But, for western anglers, fishing both banks is nearly impossible; during runoff, wading out in the current and casting back toward the bank is often unsafe due to high water and fast flow. It's easy to see why a boat becomes an important aspect of fishing such waters.

Many of the tactics in this book require no real modifications for float-fishing situations—just remember to adjust your retrieves or presentation angles based on how fast you're floating. If you're really cooking along in the current, cast more ahead of the boat so that that your fly remains longer where it needs to be before you zoom past it and have to strip behind you. If you are not floating so fast or are lucky and have a fishing buddy who was born to back-row, then you can fish in a more perpendicular manner to the centerline of the boat. Keep in mind that if you plan to dredge or dead-drift your flies while float-fishing, you and the rower must be on the same page. Float-fishing is a team effort, especially when fishing streamers.

Wading is not a team effort. It is you, the river, and the big trout. Whether you are on a small stream or large, fishing the bank you're standing on is its own challenge.

When wading, it is important to imagine your back-cast before you make it. You do not always have to look behind you, but it helps. Master the roll cast and the steeple cast. These two casts keep your fly line high and away from any bank-side obstructions.

When standing on the near bank and fishing upstream, your casting hand comes into play. Naturally, it is easier to fish the bank that is not closest to your casting arm. I like to solve this problem a few ways. Ideally, you should learn to cast with your weak arm and manage line with your normal casting arm. This takes time to master, and if you can, great. But, if switching casting arms is not an option, simply change how you would fish the bank: Instead of fishing up and across, switch and fish downstream.

On small meadow streams, you may not have to wade, but be prepared, as wading out even 5 feet will increase your chance for success. Fish downstream at an angle toward the far bank. By doing this, you are able to vary your retrieves. Experiment with a few things. For instance, let the fly swing out in the current before you begin a retrieve, or cast the fly onto the bank and slowly strip it off before going into a retrieve. When fishing downstream to a deeper hole or cutbank, stack your fly line so the fly will get deeper. When fishing the middle of the river into a current that will bring the fly *back* to the bank, simply roll cast the fly or try a backhanded cast out into the current.

By fishing downstream, you can cover a lot of water. Make a few retrieves in one spot, then take a few steps downstream while you make your quick false casts—remember, keep that fly in the water!

You will find that wading and fishing downstream is very similar to streamer fishing from a driftboat. Wading while walking *upstream*, though, presents a different set of challenges. Casting may seem easier, but it is often hard to get the right action in your fly.

The first adjustment you must make is to speed up your retrieve. When you are casting upstream, slack line builds quickly under your rod tip. This is about basic line management, but it is an especially important factor while streamer fishing—any slack may cost you a big fish. When wading upstream and fishing to a bank on your near side, cast onto the bank, throw a

STREAMER FISHING TECHNIQUES AND TACTICS

small upstream mend in the line, strip the fly off the bank, and begin your retrieve. Follow this rhythm, walking upstream a few steps between each cast; you can cover a lot of water this way. If you are planning to dredge or dead-drift, it is crucial you throw a lot of stack mends in the fly line so the flies get down and are not pulled in the current.

A benefit of fishing upstream is that you will get a long drift. As your fly and fly line float past you, do not pick them up to recast, let them drift out downstream of you. As the end of the drift nears, let the fly swing in the current and slowly raise the rod before you recast. Expect a hit during this lift—this is the lift I talked about earlier—as many fish will hit as a fly is rising in the current.

The skills in this chapter are a blend of old and new techniques. When applied to various fishing situations with the knowledge you already have, hooking and landing a fish on a streamer should not only be easier, but more enjoyable. The whole point of going fishing is to have fun. The beauty of fishing streamers for trout is that there is something for everyone—the joy of casting, the creation of new patterns, the problem-solving nature of reading water and changing conditions, and the heart-pounding excitement of seeing a big trout chase a fly.

CHAPTER FOUR

TOOLS OF THE TRADE: EQUIPMENT AND FLIES FOR STREAMER FISHING

RODS

For streamer fishing, any rod will get the job done. But, in order to get the most enjoyment from fishing big flies and, hopefully, catching big fish, it is essential to learn the differences between what types of rods will help and those that will make your angling time more frustrating.

For most streamer fishing, whether wading or fishing from boats, aim for an 8- to 9-foot rod. If you fish primarily southern or eastern waters with lots of overhead cover, you might want to consider a shorter rod, but anything shorter than 7½ feet makes it tough to cast bigger flies. Line weight is debatable, but for larger western rivers, do not head for the water with a rod less than a five-weight and never above an eight-weight. Split that difference, and a six-weight or mid-flex seven-weight will work. When I plan to streamer fish all day, I carry three rods with me: a tip-flex five-weight, a high mid-flex six-weight, and a lower mid-flex seven-weight. When friends cast my seven-weight, they consider it slow, but I tell them that when I am fishing a heavier rod for trout, one that is mid-flex doesn't make me feel like I'm casting a brute all day. My seven-weight casts 40–50 feet of line just fine with minimal false casts. Why bother with something more cumbersome just because it's faster?

99

With rods and rod action, it really is a matter of personal preference—cast a rod before you buy it and fish with it. Be sure to try a rod with sink-tip and sinking lines in addition to your standing floating lines before you buy it. In summary, choose a rod for streamer fishing in the lower line weight range that has a tip-flex action. For higher line weights (7- to 8-weight), choose a rod that you will enjoy fishing, but a mid-flex action is what I suggest.

REELS

There is no perfect reel for streamer fishing. You can spend a fortune and get a great reel, and you can spend a reasonable amount, say $100 to $200, and get a great reel, as well. For trout fishing, I am not as convinced you need to have a large-arbor reel as I am for saltwater angling, but I do like this type for trout fishing for one main reason—line memory. Trout typically live in cold climates, and cold weather and line memory go hand in hand. A large-arbor reel will save you time and a little frustration each time you fish. Do not go throw away your small-arbor reel, just be sure you stretch out your line to remove memory before you fish. This will make casting and managing the line much easier.

I am also a believer in disc drag systems when fishing big flies to big fish. A click-and-pawl drag system will work, but a disc drag handles two key features better: start-up speed and adjusting the drag while fighting a fish. Start-up speed is the inertia required to

Battenkill Large Arbor Fly Reel

TOOLS OF THE TRADE

engage the drag system. Modern disc drag reels have a start-up speed that gradually applies more pressure until it reaches its setting. Click-and-pawl systems do not, having instead notches in the pawl that apply the same pressure.

When fishing, I like to set my disc drag a little lower than I want because of the start-up inertia to engage the drag system. When the fight is on and I need more drag, I can adjust as needed. This goes against some conventional wisdom, but if I always followed the standard, I would still be catching 10-inch trout on #12 Royal Coachmans.

A final consideration when choosing a reel is to make sure it can hold at least 100 yards of backing and your fly line. And if you plan to fish streamers often (and with your new knowledge, I bet you will), purchase a few extra spools. Extra spools are essential to the streamer angler, as they allow you to carry floating, sinking, and sink-tip lines.

LINES

Fly line selection is perhaps the most misunderstood aspect of streamer fishing. I've had some great days streamer fishing using all the line types. When I look back on the greatest days of streamer fishing, I was using a floating line. But, if I look back at the biggest fish I've caught, they were hooked while fishing full-sinking lines. It is safe to say you will need at least two and probably three types of lines to effectively fish streamers *and* catch fish on them.

- *Full-sinking* lines have an undeserved stigma about them. Most trout anglers feel sinking lines are either too hard to fish or not worthwhile. They have a fair argument, as many smaller trout waters do not need to be fished with full-sinking lines. I've fished with many Midwestern anglers who come prepared with sinking lines and know how to fish them, but in Montana, where I grew up, I did not seriously fish with a sinking line until I guided in Chile for a winter.

Orvis Superfast Sinking Wonderline

When fishing full-sinking lines, you will find they are actually quite easy to cast. At first they pull the rod tip in an erratic fashion, but only because they load the rod quicker than a floating line. Full-sinking lines are more difficult to mend, but in most streamer fishing situations, and especially those when you are using a full-sinking line, you will not mend that often.

One problem I've seen beginners struggle with when fishing sinking lines is the tendency of these lines to knot and tangle. Do not let any of these tangles or knots tighten, as they are ex-

Orvis Wonderline Advantage Intermediate Sinking Line

tremely hard to remove. I suggest using lines with Wonderline™ coating, as they are less likely to tangle.

- *Sink-tip* lines are good compromise between floating and full-sinking, but they also serve a very unique purpose. I like fishing clear-tip lines on tailwaters or rivers that have lots of fish feeding on flats or shelves.

One of my favorite fishing times is during April and May on the Missouri, when post-spawn rainbows and big browns are feeding in shallow water. A sink tip allows the fly to get down fast,

Orvis Streamer Stripper Sink Tip

and an unweighted fly fished with either the jerk-strip or strip-down method can produce great results. Fishing unweighted flies on sink-tip lines is a deadly technique and should be practiced by every serious streamer angler. A specialized sink tip is the Orvis Streamer Stripper™. This line has a 4-foot mini sink tip and is great for shallow flats and fish grouped in pods.

- *Floating lines* are still very useful when fishing streamers. During July and August, I rarely fish streamers on anything *but* a floating line. However, that's on Montana's Missouri River, where fish of

Orvis Olive Dun WF Wonderline Floating Fly Line

all size feed in various depths of water. On many eastern and Midwestern rivers, floating lines may be used year-round, as the fish you are targeting are not in deep water. A basic, weight-forward floating line should be used, though I do make one adjustment and sometimes fish a bass taper. This allows big flies to turn over more easily, and the extended rear taper allows for easier shooting. I've found beginning anglers can get more casts in throughout a day of fishing when using a bass taper—it just takes less effort to get the fly out to the fish.

A final word on line selection. Over-lining is a common practice among many streamer anglers. If you have a five-weight tip-flex fly rod, consider fishing a 6-weight, weight-forward floating line. The heavy line loads the rod faster and requires less false casting, which means your fly will get to the fish faster and more often. However, if you are fishing a rod shorter than 8½ feet, you might *not* want to over-line your rod, because mending might be too much of a chore.

LEADERS

One of the things I truly enjoy about streamer fishing is the lack of a long or complex leader system. Most trout that attack a streamer will not be leader shy or even be concerned about the leader—they're intent on whacking your big offering. Because your fly has action or is moving, it is not affected by the drifting currents except when dead-drifting or dredging. In

Orvis Super Strong Tapered Leader

those instances, leader composition is important and should be rigged similarly to that of standard tandem nymphing.

There is no need to fish a leader any longer than 6 feet. You might find a longer leader necessary *if* the presentation of the fly or fly line is causing the trout to become nervous or edgy, but if that is the case, the fish will probably not hit your streamer anyway. Streamer leaders must be heavy enough to turn over a big fly, and if the length is kept under 6 feet, you can fish a tippet of eight- to twelve-pound test. If you tie your own leaders, the general formula is 18–24 inches of twenty- to thirty-pound butt section and 10–18 inches of fifteen-pound test, then your tippet section, which can be 12–16 inches of eight- to twelve-pound test.

This is a simple formula and requires little adjustment, but be sure your tippet material is abrasion resistant—you will be dragging it across rocks, logs, and the teeth of big trout! Fluorocarbon leaders offer tougher abrasion resistance, better sink rates, and lower visibility than nylon leaders when fishing streamers. For these reasons, I recommend using them (as well as fluorocarbon tippets).

FLY PATTERNS: THE MOST EFFECTIVE FLIES

In the current world of fly fishing, an angler can be quickly overwhelmed by the number of patterns available. And, if you are fly tier, your brain can fast go numb with the massive amounts of new and old tying material on the market. You can also go bankrupt if you tried to stock your box or tying bench with all that's available.

When selecting flies for streamer fishing, take a few things into consideration. Your first priority should be the area of the country and the type of stream you will be fishing. For instance, larger rivers usually require bigger flies, and smaller rivers require smaller or sparser imitations. Second, take into account the main

TOOLS OF THE TRADE

food source on that river or stream; if you are fishing a sculpin pattern in a river where crayfish make up the primary food source, you might want to rethink your strategy. Last, consider the immediate fishing conditions. Are you fishing deep runs? Muddy water due to a heavy rain or runoff? Or is the focus shallow banks or flats?

Fly size, of course, is also a consideration. The patterns I suggest can be fished with much success in a wide variety of sizes. For larger rivers, I usually fish with nothing smaller than a #6. For small creeks, I let the average size of its trout determine the size of fly; if I know a tiny creek has 18- to 22-inch fish, I will still fish a #2 fly.

Before we look at what patterns work best in various regions of the country, let's break down the flies based on the food they represent. I have not specified bead-head, weighted, or unweighted, because you can get all these patterns in various configurations and you'll fish the appropriate one depending on the sink rate you need.

Baitfish: Darters, Dace, Trout, and Other Small Fish

Most baitfish patterns have several things in common. The best patterns have something that resembles eyes, possess vibrant or blended colors, are tied with materials that "breathe" or have a nice action when stripped, and will cast well. Over the past ten years, baitfish patterns have been revolutionized with the advent of new tying materials. Because of this, the following list of effective baitfish patterns includes some oldies but goodies, as well as some very modern patterns.

1. Bead-Head Lite Brite Zonker

2. Cone-Head Double Bunny

3. Matuka

4. Clouser's Deep Minnow

5. Orange Blossom Special Fly

6. Black-Nosed Dace

Sculpins and Bullheads

As previously discussed, sculpins make up a large percentage of a trout's diet and an even larger percentage of available food in most streams. Their patterns should be an essential component of your tackle.

Sculpin patterns must have a large head and slender body. They must also have good action when stripped. They can have either vibrant colors or colors similar to the naturals they imitate. You can typically fish a sculpin pattern that is quite large, 2½–4 inches, because big fish will hunt and ambush sculpins this size—they are that tasty.

1. Cone-Head Muddler Minnow

2. Chuck-and-Duck Sculpin

3. Black Marabou Muddler

4. Rag Sculpin

5. Wool-Head Sculpin

6. Tung-Head Muddler Minnow

7. Moto's Minnow

8. Cone-Head Zuddler

Woolly Buggers and Leeches

Woolly Bugger patterns are primarily crayfish and leech patterns, but they deserve special distinction. If I were only allowed to fish one fly for the rest of my angling life, it would be a #4 Black Woolly Bugger. The marabou tail and hackled body make this fly an all-around champion of the trout stream. There are many variations of the Woolly Bugger, and a few are listed below, but a good ol' Black, Brown, or Olive Woolly Bugger is a great pattern. All can be tied bead-head, cone-head, or unweighted.

1. Bead-Head Woolly Bugger

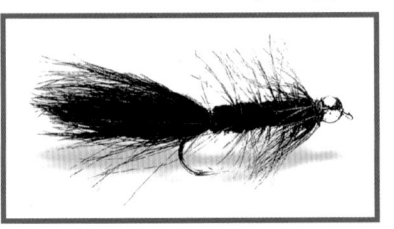

2. Cone-Head Woolly Bugger

3. Egg-Sucking Leech

4. Krystal Bugger

Crayfish

Crayfish are abundant in most trout streams. During certain times of the year, large trout will feed exclusively on crayfish. My main factors in choosing a crayfish pattern are its durability and its ease in casting.

Crayfish patterns can be fun to tie, because you are adding claws, antennae, and mono-eyes. However, I've found that often the simple crayfish patterns work just as well as the complicated and lifelike imitations.

1. Woolly Bugger

2. General Craw

3. Cone-Head Rubber Bugger

Top Regional Patterns

I am a believer that a trout is a trout, whether you are on the Delaware River or the Gunnison. Naturally, each river will have a different abundance of food. I've covered a large amount of information regarding trout food in Chapter Two, but there are some regional differences in the variations of patterns anglers should fish. For example, a Cone-Head Woolly Bugger may work wonders on the South Fork of the Snake, but it might be overkill on Vermont's White or a small stream in the Blue Ridge Mountains. Therefore I have listed top patterns for the various regions of the U.S.

Eastern

1. Black Woolly Bugger

2. Lite Brite Zonker

3. Black Marabou Muddler

4. Black-Nosed Dace

5. Grey Ghost

6. Cone-Head Zuddler

7. Mickey Finn

8. Egg-Sucking Leech

9. Clouser Minnow

Southern

1. Cone-Head Zuddler

2. Grey Ghost

3. General Craw

4. Egg-Sucking Leech

5. Black Woolly Bugger

6. Olive Woolly Bugger

Midwestern

1. Black Woolly Bugger

2. Wool-Head Sculpin

3. Cone-Head Muddler Minnow

4. Egg-Sucking Leech

5. Moto's Minnow

6. Cone-Head Zuddler

7. Rag Sculpin

8. Clouser Minnow

9. Black-Nosed Dace

Rocky Mountains

1. Black or Olive Woolly Bugger

2. Lite Brite Zonker

3. Cone-Head Marabou Muddler

4. Orange Blossom

5. Matuka

6. Cone-Head Rubber Bugger

Pacific Northwest and California

1. Egg-Sucking Leech

2. Black Woolly Bugger

3. Grey Ghost

4. Black-Nosed Dace

5. Clouser Minnow

6. Cone-Head Marabou Muddler

7. Chuck-and-Duck Sculpin

8. Wool-Head Sculpin

9. Strip Tease

CHAPTER FIVE

A PERFECT DAY OF STREAMER FISHING

The best day of streamer fishing usually begins the night before: sorting out your fishing buddies for the day, making sure the house chores are complete, getting to bed at a reasonable hour. The meeting time and place are arranged before the alarm is set, and the most important detail of them all—who's responsible for bringing the beer—has been settled on. You even find some time to tie a few Bead-Head Double Bunnies, maybe even a couple Black Rubber-Legged Woolly Buggers. As an indulgence to your tying ability and to support your local fly shop, tomorrow, on your way out of town, you will buy some Trick or Treats, as well.

The next morning, your perfect day of streamer fishing gets off on the right foot. Because he or she cares about you going hungry, your spouse has brewed a fresh pot of coffee, made an omelet, and fried some bacon for you. After enjoying breakfast, you take your lunch, which was also packed for you, and head out to meet up with your fishing partners. Stowing your gear, you notice your pickup is covered in tiny droplets of rain; a soft drizzle is falling from the lightly overcast skies. What a day this is going to be!

On the way to the river, you talk about how you are going to only fish streamers today. "I'm going to start with one and end with one." The other anglers in the

134

car just laugh. One of them even says, "Shoot, I only fish streamers when nothing else is working. My arm just gets too tired, and those sinking lines are hard to cast." Your lack of comment and silence express your optimism for your chosen method. Thankfully, the thump of the driftboat trailer bumping onto the dirt road breaks an awkward moment.

You were not odd man out in rock-paper-scissors, so you avoid starting out on the oars. Supplied with a bellyful of home cooking, you strip line off your reel, visualizing your first cast. But wait. Your buddy in the back of the boat points out a bald eagle perched in the highest branches of a cottonwood tree. You and the eagle both have fishing on your mind.

Turning your attention back to your first cast, you strip line from the reel and let it fall at your feet. Your buddy on the oars is breathing hard as he back-rows to slow the boat for the oncoming shaded and rocky bank. You pick out a current seam behind a rock. From the change in color downstream of the rock, you can tell there is slight drop-off. With one false cast, you drop your fly barely on the bank, strip once to get it in the water, then jerk-strip about five times. From the depths, like a firework explosion, a big brown lunges at your fly—but he hits so fast you don't get a hook in him.

It would be just a little too good to hook a pig on your first cast, right?

Your buddy on the oars hoots; the guy in the back gawks and says, "Holy moly, what was that? He was huge!" You are still recovering from that heart-stopper of a hit. After getting hold of yourself, you see another

A PERFECT DAY OF STREAMER FISHING

likely spot—the current bounces off a fallen log and boils behind it. You quickly roll cast and go into your backcast, dropping the fly just in front of the log. Before the oarsmen can say "Nice shot," you've already gotten in five line strips, but nothing chases. You pick your line right up and into another backcast and shoot your line and fly into the slack behind the log, adding in a tuck cast to drive the fly down. *Plunk*. The fly lands. You get one line strip in and . . . *ka-boom!* The slack water behind the log erupts into waves and splashing water. Your instincts now kick in, and you side-strip and set the hook. You got him!

"Oh baby!" your buddy in the back hollers. "He's a whale!" The oarsman grunts as he digs into his backrow, "We're gonna be awhile." After a valiant fight of leaps, long runs, and deep dives, you bring the monster alongside the boat and land it. With the oarsman netting the fish, you lean over the side and gently cradle your trout, lifting it just out of the water. Your buddy in the back takes several pictures, then one more as you slide your trophy back into the river's current.

"I'm cutting off this #14 Trude and putting on a Bugger," says the angler in the back. "What do you think about trying a sinking line?"

What a start to a perfect day of streamer fishing! The rest of the day, the three of you take turns rowing and hooking fish. Late in the afternoon, the clouds break and the sun lifts, but the fish are still on the prowl for streamers. In fact, one of your friends catches the biggest fish of the day in the heart of a shallow flat around 3:00 PM. The best part, he said, was seeing the monster brown chase down his White Trick or Treat. "I just kept stripping and stripping, and finally the big pig attacked it," he said in wonder.

On the last bend before the boat ramp, you are on the oars and your friends are casting toward the bank. You take a quick glance over your shoulder to examine a nice riffle. You tell your friend in the back, who is focused on the bank but hasn't moved a fish in a bit, to drop a cast right in the heart of that riffle. He picks up, water-hauling, and shoots a little line on his back-cast—which *is* his presentation cast—into the riffle. While his fly is in the air, the bow angler shouts, "Oh! Almost got . . . *yeah*! He just nailed it twice! Fish on!"

"Nice work," you say, digging in with the oars. "We'll land him at the boat ramp."

Just as the bow angler's nice fish jumps, the back angler hooks up. "Bam! Got him!" he exclaims. Line peels out of the stern angler's reel as the fish turns into the main current and heads downstream. "I gotta let him run," your buddy says.

"No worries, *mon*," you assure him in your best island accent. "We'll land him at the boat ramp, too!"

As you back the stern of the boat onto the ramp, the front and back anglers hop out. You drag the boat up on the bank, hop out with the net, and land both fish in it. "A great brown and a great 'bow," you admire aloud. You give the net to your friends and take a picture of the two of them standing side by side, each holding big trout.

Did I mention this was a perfect day of streamer fishing?

CHAPTER SIX

SOME FINAL THOUGHTS AND THE FLY-FISHING MENTALITY

Fly fishing is a wonderful pastime. Over the years, it has taken me to many wonderful places the world over. In those travels, people always ask me which is my favorite species of fish to catch. My response is always the same: whatever I am fishing for at the moment. As for my favorite *place* to fish . . . . Well, while I have to admit there are those cold and dark winter days where I long for a saltwater flat and a blended, fruity drink with plenty of rum, my heart has always held a special place for the trout streams of Montana.

I've felt blessed to have grown up within an hour's drive of the Yellowstone, Madison, and Gallatin rivers. For me, fly fishing is simply a way of enjoying the gift of being able to be outside, on a river, and feeling connected to our natural world. Thankfully, through the conservation efforts of many, the practice of catch-and-release angling, and continued education of both anglers and the general public, we can experience wonderful outings like the one described in Chapter Five.

However, the world is changing (though, unfortunately, there are no new trout streams being created), and a better understanding of fishing and the enjoyment we get from it needs to occur. We, as anglers, should not judge the worth of a day's fishing by the number of fish caught. Rather, for some, the day will be accounted for by seeing a certain kind of bird. Or by the chance encounter with a pristine pool, crystal-clear blue in the morning sun. Or maybe it will be just because we were able to get away from our busy lives and spend a day on the water.

I try to deter anglers from counting their catches—why try to quantify an experience that really cannot be measured in numbers? For a busy mother or father, their best fishing experience may be when they can finally take their son or daughter on a day- or week-long fishing trip. Even if the pair do not catch a single fish, they were able to get away together. To me, that is the beauty of fly fishing. There is enjoyment in it for all.

Fly fishing for trout, and especially streamer fishing for trout, has given me many great memories, close friends, distant friends I don't see enough, humility, ego boosts, and the occasional rare moment when I am able to forget all the worries of the world and simply enjoy the river against my legs, the rush of blood in my veins the moment a fish is hooked, and the cherry-on-top that is releasing a beautiful trout back to the water.

SOME FINAL THOUGHTS

INDEX

A

Across-and-downstream, 67–69
Aggression
  trout, 25
Anglers
  dry-fly, 4
  nymph, 4
  streamer
    logjams, 35
Angling
  catch-and-release, 140
Aquatic worms, 23
Atmospheric conditions
  streamer fishing, 136

B

Backcasting, 138
Back eddies, 32
Bait fish, 11–13, 110–112
  rivers, 12
  trout, 13
Banks
  rip-rap, 28–33
    elements, 31–32
  undercut, 6
Barbless hooks, 94
Battenkill Large Arbor Fly Reel,
    101
Beaching
  big fish, 92
Bead-Head #12, 74
Bead-Head dropper, 80
Bead-Head Lite Brite Zonker
  photograph, 111
Bead-Head Woolly Bugger
  photograph, 116

Beartrap Canyon, 19
Beginners
  fishing sinking lines, 104
Behavior
  trout, 7–10
Belly, 64–65
  construction, 65
  retrieve
    illustration, 64
Big brown trout
  illustration, 12
Big fish
  beaching, 92
  fighting, 81–83
  hooking, 81–83
  landing them, 91
  netting, 91
  releasing, 93
  rising movement, 90
  survival, 93
Bighorn River, 31
Birds, 11
Black Marabou Muddler
  illustration, 114
Black-Nosed Dace, 19
  photograph, 112, 121, 127, 131
Black Woolly Bugger, 13
  photograph, 120, 124, 125, 130
Bluntnose trout, 16
Boat(s)
  advancements, 67
Boat fishing
  streamer fishing, 99
  wading
    differences, 95
Boulders, 28–33

Boulders *(cont.)*
  holding patterns, 30
Bozeman, Montana, 19
Brown, Duke, 20, 72
Brown trout
  illustration, 12
  large, 16
Brown Woolly Bugger, 20, 24
Buggers
  dead-drifting, 75
Bullheads, 113–115
Burrowing
  fish, 89

C
Casting. *See also* Roll cast
  angle
    sidearm, 52
  drifts, 71
  false, 42–43
  full-sinking lines, 104
  rhythm, 49
  ruckus, 49–50
    illustration, 50
  skills
    philosophy, 42–44
  skip, 50–52
    illustration, 51
  stroke, 42
  hand position illustrations, 43
  tuck, 49–50
    illustration, 50
Catch-and-release angling, 140
Chuck-and-Duck Sculpin
  photograph, 113, 132
Classic swing method
  fly line, 68
Click-and-pawl systems, 102
Clouser Minnow
  photograph, 122, 127, 132

Clouser's Deep Minnow, 112
Comfort range
  trout, 9
Cone-Head Double Bunny
  photograph, 111
Cone-Head Marabou Muddler
  photograph, 128, 132
Cone-Head Muddler Minnow
  photograph, 113, 125
Cone-Head Rubber Bugger
  photograph, 119, 129
Cone-Head Woolly Bugger
  photograph, 116
Cone-Head Zuddler
  photograph, 115, 121, 123, 126
Cover
  examples, 6
  fish, 5
Crawdads, 21. *See also* Crayfish
Crawfish, 21. *See also* Crayfish
Crayfish, 11, 19–22, 21, 117–118
  patterns, 22, 118
  photograph, 20
Currents
  rising
    push-up, 34–35
  river, 86–91
  river tides, 29
Cutbanks, 39–40
  illustration, 40

D
Dace, 16, 18–19, 110–112
  Black-Nosed, 19
    photograph, 112, 121, 127,
      131
  Canada, 18
  U.S., 18
Darters, 15–16
  perch family, 15
Dead-drifting, 72–74

142   INDEX

Buggers, 75
dredging
  differences, 77
fly line swing, 75
illustration, 73
  big flies, 73
rod positioning, 75
stack mending, 98
stack mends, 98
two-fly rigs, 74–75
Deep pools, 39–40
  fishing streamers, 5
Delaware River, 119
Disc drag systems, 100
Diving
  fish, 89
Dombrowski, Chris, 17
Down-and-dirty technique,
  76–78
Downstream fishing
  wading, 97
Drag tightness
  fish movement, 88
Dredging, 76–78
  dead-drifting
    differences, 77
  illustration, 76
  methods, 77
  sink-tip line, 77
  stack mending, 98
  stack mends, 98
Drifts
  cast, 71
Drop-offs, 39–40
  fishing streamers, 5
Dropper fly, 80
Dropper loop, 80
Dry-fly anglers, 4, 15
Dry-fly fishing, 8
  dead-drifting technique, 74
Ducklings, 24

E
Eddies
  back, 32
Egg-Sucking Leech
  photograph, 117, 122, 124, 126,
    130
Equipment, 83–85
  streamer fishing, 99–134

F
False casting, 42
  reduction, 43
Feeding rhythms
  trout, 7–10
Fence lines, 37
  illustration, 36
Fences, 33–37
  western rivers, 37
Fighting
  big fish, 81–83
  illustration, 87, 89
Fingerling trout, 4, 26
First cast
  streamer fishing, 135
Fish
  away movement, 87
  burrowing, 89
  cover, 5
  diving, 89
  fighting tactics
    illustration, 87, 89
  head control, 83
  head relationship, 81
  holding period illustration,
    31
  holding periods, 30
  movement
    drag tightness, 88
  photographing, 93
  pre-spawn periods, 30
Fishing. *See also* specific type

Fishing *(cont.)*
  sinking lines
    beginners, 104
  streamers
    deep pools, 5
    drop-offs, 5
    tippets, 84
  unhooking yourself, 94
Flats, 37–39
  water conditions, 38
Flies
  dropper, 80
  patterns
    effectiveness, 109–110
  selection
    streamer fishing, 109
  streamer fishing, 99
Float fishing
  tactics, 95–98
  team effort, 96
Floating lines, 106
Fly-fishing
  knowledge, 42
  mentality, 138–139
  running fish, 86
Fly line
  selection
    streamer fishing, 102
  swing
    dead-drifting, 75
Fly-tying materials, 66
Frogs, 11, 24
Full-sinking lines, 103, 104

G
Gear
  advancements, 66
General Craw
  photograph, 118, 123
Gradient changes, 40

Grey Ghost
  photograph, 121, 123, 131

H
Hand positioning
  for rods, 53
Hare's Ear #16, 20
Haul
  definition, 44
Head
  control
    fish, 83
  relationship
    fish, 81
Hellgrammites, 11
Holding periods
  fish, 30
    illustration, 31
Holter Dam, 27
Hooking
  big fish, 81–83
Hooks
  barbless, 94
Hook set
  side-strip, 82
Hunger maximization
  trout, 25

J
Jack retrieve, 62–63
Jerk-strip
  fly action, 61
Jerk-strip retrieve, 60–62
  illustration, 61
  positioning, 60
Jigging, 63–65

K
Knot leader systems, 80

Knowledge
  fly-fishing, 42
Krystal Bugger
  photograph, 117

L

Lampreys, 22–23
  microscope view, 23
Landing
  big fish, 91
Large brown trout, 16
Large white suckers, 16
Leaders, 107–109
Leader system, 107
Ledges, 40
Leeches, 11, 22–23, 116–117
  imitation, 22
Line-only strip method, 54–56
Lines, 102–109
  handling
    trigger finger, 55
Lite Brite Zonker
  photograph, 120, 128
Lobster
  poor man's, 21
Logjams, 33–37
  fishing, 35
  illustration, 33
  streamer anglers, 35
Logs, 33–37
  targeting, 34
Loop
  dropper, 80

M

Marabou Muddler
  Black
    photograph, 114, 120
  Cone-Head
    photograph, 128, 132

Matthews, Craig, 24
Matuka
  photograph, 111, 129
Meadow streams
  wading, 97
Mending. *See* Stack mending
Mentality
  fly-fishing, 140–141
Mice, 24
Mickey Finn
  photograph, 122
Mindset
  streamer fishing, 94
  stream fishing, 27–28
Minnow
  Clouser
    photograph, 122, 127, 132
  Clouser's Deep, 112
  Cone-Head Muddler
    photograph, 113, 125
  Moto's
    photograph, 115, 126
  Tung-Head Muddler, 115
Missouri, 27
Missouri River, 8, 106
Moto's Minnow
  photograph, 115, 126
Movement
  trout, 86
Mudbugs, 21. *See also* Crayfish
Mudpuppies, 21. *See also*
        Crayfish
Munson, Garrett, 8, 27

N

Nehring, Jon, 60
Netting
  big fish, 91
Nymph anglers, 4
Nymphing techniques, 74

O

Olive Hare's Ear #16, 20
Olive Rubber-Legged Woolly
    Bugger #4, 1
Olive Woolly Bugger, 20
  photograph, 124, 128
Olive Woolly Bugger #2, 5
Orange Blossom
  photograph, 112, 129
Orvis Fly-Casting Guide, 42
*Orvis Guide to Reading Trout
    Streams,* 26
Orvis Olive Du WF Wonderline
    Floating Fly Line
  illustration, 106
*Orvis Pocket Guide to Approach
    and Presentation,* 26
Orvis Streamer Stripper, 106
Orvis Streamer Stripper Sink Tip
  illustration, 105
Orvis Superfast Sinking
    Wonderline, 103
Orvis Super Strong Tapered
    Leader
  illustration, 108
Orvis Wonderline Advantage
    Intermediate Sinking Line,
    104
Over-lining, 107

P

Perch family, 15
Percidae, 15
Photographing fish, 93
Pools
  deep, 39–40
Poor man's lobster, 21. *See also*
    Crayfish
Predator
  trout, 3–25

Pre-spawn periods
  fish, 30
Prey
  trout, 3–25
Primary food source
  trout, 10–11

R

Rag Sculpin
  photograph, 114, 127
Rainbow trout
  feeding habits, 12
  fingerling, 26
  illustration, 12
Reeling
  streamer fishing, 100
Reels, 100–102
  choices, 102
Releasing
  big fish, 93
Retrieving
  jack, 63
  jerk-strip, 60–62
    illustration, 61
    positioning, 60
  saltwater jack, 62–63
  side-strip, 58–60
    fishing situations, 58
    illustration, 59
    strip down, 58
  streamer fishing, 52, 66
  strip-down, 56–58
    illustration, 56
    refinement aspects, 57
    speed effectiveness, 57
  variances, 63
Riffles, 6
  illustration, 7
Rip-rap banks, 28–33
  elements, 31–32

Rising currents
push-up, 34–35
Rising movement
big fish, 90
River currents, 86–91
River current tides, 29
Rocks, 28–33
holding patterns, 30
Rods, 99–100
action, 100
advancements, 66
angle
illustration, 83
fish control, 85
hand positioning, 53
positioning
dead-drifting, 75
tip action
illustration, 84
Rod tip
positioning, 53
Roll cast, 42, 46–49, 138
definition, 47
execution, 47
pickup, 46–49
unsnagging, 46–49, 48
illustration, 48
Rubber Bugger
Cone-Head
photograph, 119, 129
Ruckus cast, 49–50
illustration, 50
Runs, 37–39

S

Sabota, Andrew, 34
Salamanders, 11
Saltwater canals, 62
Saltwater jack retrieve, 62–63
illustration, 62

Sculpin, 13–15, 113–115
baitfish, 14
Chuck-and-Duck
photograph, 113, 132
flies
size range, 15
growth size, 14
pectoral fins, 14
Rag
photograph, 114, 127
Wool-Head
photograph, 114, 125, 133
Shelves, 37–39
fish holding, 38
Shiners, 19
Sidearm casting angle, 52
Side-strip hook set, 82
Side-strip retrieve, 58–60
fishing situations, 58
illustration, 59
strip down, 58
Simple strip, 54–56
illustration, 55
Sink-tip, 105
line
dredging, 77
Skip cast, 50–52
illustration, 51
Speed retrieval
streamer fishing, 54
Stack mending, 69–72
application, 71
dead-drifting, 98
dredging, 98
illustration of, 70
success, 72
Streamer(s)
targeting trout, 4
Streamer anglers
logjams, 35

Streamer fishing
  action, 54
  atmospheric conditions,
    134
  boat fishing, 99
  equipment, 99–135
  first cast, 137
  flies, 99
  fly line selection, 102
  fly selection, 109
  mindset, 94
  physical aspects, 2
  reeling, 100
  retrieval, 66
  retrieving, 52
  speed retrieval, 54
  success measurement, 134–139,
  tactics, 41–98
  techniques, 41–98, 66–67
  trout, 141
  variation methods, 2
  wading, 99
Streamer rigs
  two-fly
    illustration, 79
Streamer weather, 8
Stream reading
  location, 26–40
Strip-down retrieve, 56–58
  illustration, 56
  refinement aspects, 57
  speed effectiveness, 57
Stripping, 42
Strip Tease
  photograph, 133
Structure
  definition, 28
Success measurement
  streamer fishing, 134–139

Suckers
  large white, 16
  young white, 16
Survival
  big fish, 93
Swing drift
  line stacking, 71
Swing method, 67–69
  casts, 67
  fly line, 68
  stack mending, 69
  wading, 69

T
Tactics
  float fishing, 95–98
  streamer fishing, 41–98
  wading, 95–98
Tandem rigs, 78–81
Tan Hare's Ear, 20–21
Tarpon, 7–8
Team effort
  float fishing, 96
  wading, 96
Techniques
  streamer fishing, 41–98,
    66–67
Tides
  river current, 29
Tippets
  fishing streamers, 84
Tracking, 78
Trigger finger, 53
  line handling, 55
Trophy landing, 91–93
Trout, 7–8, 110–112
  aggression, 25
  baitfish, 13
  behavior, 7–10

big brown
  illustration, 12
bluntnose, 16
comfort range, 9
feeding rhythms, 7–10
fingerling rainbow, 26
hunger maximization, 25
large brown, 16
movement, 86
predator, 3–25
predator analogy, 3
prey, 3–25
primary food source, 10–11
rainbow
  feeding habits, 12
  fingerling, 26
  illustration, 12
rip-rap eddy, 32
streamer fishing, 139
weather changes, 9
yearling
  illustration, 17
Trude #14, 136
Tuck cast, 49–50
  illustration, 50
Tung-Head Muddler Minnow, 115
Two-fly rigs, 78–81
  dead-drifting, 74–75
Two-fly streamer rigs
  illustration, 79

U
Undercut banks, 6
Unhooking yourself
  fishing, 94
Unsnagging roll cast, 46–49
Upstream fishing
  advantages, 98

V
Vikings, 1

W
Wading
  boat fishing
    differences, 95
  downstream fishing, 97
  meadow streams, 97
  streamer fishing, 99
  tactics, 95–98
  team effort, 96
  upstream fishing, 97
Water conditions
  flats, 38
Water current seams, 36
Water haul, 44–46
  great technique, 45
  illustration, 45
Weather
  streamer, 8
  trout, 9
White suckers
  large, 16
  young, 16
White Woolly Bugger, 13
Wind
  feeding, 10
  hunting, 10
Wool-Head Sculpin
  photograph, 114, 125, 133
Woolly Bugger, 80, 116–117
  Black, 13, 120, 124, 125, 130
  Bead-Head, 116
  Brown, 20, 24
  Cone-Head, 116
  Olive, 20, 124, 128
  olive rubber-legged #4, 1
  White, 13

Woolly Bugger #2
    Olive, 5
Woolly Bugger #4, 39, 74
Worm dropper, 24
Worms, 23–24
    aquatic, 23

Y
Yearling trout
    illustration, 17
Young white suckers, 16